PHANTOM PHENOMENA

PHANTOM PHENOMENA

TALES OF THE WORLD'S MOST TERRIFYING AND SUPERNATURAL EVENTS

DARKNESS PREVAILS

castle

I dedicate this book to my wife
—who supports me through all the nightmares, both fun and frightening—and to
the amazing folks who took the time to share these stories with us.

CONTENTS

☠

INTRODUCTION

N early two decades ago, I sat bored in my middle school's computer lab, having just finished my typing exercises. Our teacher walked out of the room for the remainder of the period, so of course, I browsed the web (which we were not allowed to do during class).

Somehow, I found myself on forums where people shared their eyewitness accounts of supernatural events. It fascinated me. Sure, I'd heard of ghosts and Bigfoot from TV; however, reading allegedly authentic accounts directly from real people struck a spark in me.

Now, I'm nearly thirty, sharing such stories to millions of people around the world through YouTube and podcasts alike. I never expected to be where I am today.

We all remember when we discovered that curiosity for things that go bump in the night. We paranormal fans often crave a wicked encounter of our own, searching for a new magic. What if Barbara down the road really did see a Dogman while driving home? What if Uncle Henry told the truth about a demonic figure appearing in his room? The idea that these entities could be real is frightening. But if Barbara's or Uncle Henry's story is true, then there's more to this world than the horrors we know all too well.

We're simply escaping from reality and hoping for the best—but instead of tales of heroism and delightful adventures, our escape happens to be hairy, fanged, or translucent (and possibly standing by your bed while you sleep). So, to all the skeptics, be kind to those who live for nightmares.

All the stories you'll read here were submitted by those who experienced them. They survived to tell the tale, and so can you. Now, curl up, listen to the rain, and try to ignore the darkness around you, no matter how hungry it feels. Allow yourself to watch through someone else's eyes as they come face-to-horrible-face . . . *with the unexplained.*

The stories you are about to read have not been proven. Due to the number of submissions that have been collected anonymously, names and attributions have been removed unless otherwise noted.

Keep in mind: *These stories are not told through my perspective, but through the perspective of those who experienced them or what they've heard from others.*

Some stories in this collection include mentions of suicide, violence against animals, and other adult themes. Reader discretion is advised.

PERILOUS PARKS

The stories in this section are set in national and state US parks. They involve the disturbing things seen within the seemingly endless wilderness that makes up these public lands. When the terrors of Mother Nature's dark side lay their eyes on you out there, you'd better hope you're a fast runner. But, run too far and the woods will engulf you, making you another missing person among many. More than one thousand people disappear in national and state parks every year, with some cases remaining unsolved. Some involve disturbing and mysterious circumstances: clothes found neatly folded; strange, hairy creatures sighted; and sudden bad weather to erase any trace of the vanished.

Visit these beautiful public lands, but respect their guidelines and markers. Bringing another GPS tracking device is essential; don't rely solely on your smartphone. Bring family or friends to reduce risk, and keep an eye on the last person in line. One moment, they might be gone—or worse, you might find an extra member has joined your crew. An individual who doesn't quite look or act very human.

At that point, you can only pray your case doesn't go unsolved.

WEATHERMAN AND THE CUYAHOGA VALLEY BUZZER

Far from civilization, rain beats down on the fabric of your tent.
You try to find comfort in the noise emitting from your radio. But as the
night carries on, something easily strips away this comfort.

FIELD NOTES
Location: Cuyahoga Valley National Park, USA
Date/Time: Unknown—but nice enough weather to go camping
Atmosphere: Rainy, damp, buzzy

This story was not told to me by a hiker, like most other stories I've heard. Instead, I witnessed these events firsthand. This encounter occurred very close to my home woods of Ohio, way up north in Cuyahoga Valley National Park.

Cuyahoga Valley is a smaller park. It's one of the few national parks on the East Coast and doesn't get nearly as much love as it should. That said, it's somewhat of a private heaven for those of us who take the trip into the valley to escape the more populous parks.

Because of the nature of the sites in the Valley, it's best to have at least one other person with you, so you can look out for each other in the unpredictable landscape. I had ached for a return to the forest, as it had been a fair amount of time since my last excursion. Eventually, I persuaded an old friend from the area to join me on the hike. He wasn't a camper at all; 90 percent of what he carried that weekend was gear borrowed from me.

I was excited to take him on the trip with me. For those new to the world of the great outdoors, a big tradition and rite of passage for any novice outdoorsman is to earn a "trail name." This is a unique nickname given by other, more experienced hikers—usually in reference to an event at a campout or something like that. My trail name is "Spades," due to some card game fun on one of my first long hikes. I had decided to take it upon myself to find an appropriate trail name for my friend. I assumed it would be something silly, like a friend of mine whose name was "Ramen-bomben," following his creation of an instant ramen, potato, and SPAM concoction.

My hopes for a jovial, light-hearted name never came through. After the event of that night, he had forever earned the name "Weatherman." Here's why.

Weatherman and I started our trip perfectly, as many trips do. The forecast for the three-day trip was all sunny for the first two days and then a rolling storm on the last night that we may or may not get hit by, depending on our speed.

The trouble didn't start until the second night. Weatherman had brought along a small radio to check the weather. Each night before lights out, we'd listen to the scheduled segment of the serene meteorologist lady predicting the upcoming storms. On the first night, it was not a big deal at all, really: light rain on the last night and not much else. On the second night, the calm lady informed us that a heavy storm was rolling in, and accordingly, heavy rain was to be expected.

By the end of the third day's hike, the clouds above were dark and glum. The intense scent of rain hung over the entire area. Most of the other hikers in the area made the smart choice to skip that night. I, however, wanted to show Weatherman that rain doesn't always mean a bad time. To remedy the oncoming waters, we strung up the tarp that I usually slept under above Weatherman's tent, and we both stayed inside that.

Around 4 p.m. was when the water began to trickle in, and it was a full deluge only twenty minutes later. We were prepared for this; we'd eaten lunch early and got as prepared for the short walk out in the morning as possible. We hunkered down in the tent as the light outside slowly faded away.

Weatherman, in his nightly routine, flicked on his radio. This time, rather than the greeting of the soothing weather lady, the unnerving buzz of the national

Numbers stations, which transmitted encrypted codes via shortwave radio, were widely used during the Cold War for espionage. Some of these stations have stuck around, leaving rogue frequencies transmitting strange code to unsuspecting drivers. The most alarming thing about these stations is just how unknown their purpose is.

Anyone would get goosebumps while traveling on empty roads late at night, eventually hearing your soothing music transform into a creepy voice reciting a sequence of seemingly random numbers and codes. Nobody has cracked any of the codes given, nor does anyone know why they're still transmitting—or how to stop them. What are these stations transmitting? What information is being kept behind cyphers? And how many are out there, right under our noses?

weather service alert met us. You know the ones I mean, the high-pitched ones that really just shake your nerves a little bit. The warning predicted heavy rains and flash flood possibilities. We were up high on our site, so we both decided to turn in early so we could pack it out quickly in the morning.

At around 2 a.m., both Weatherman and I jolted awake in our sleeping bags. In confusion, we looked at each other. Hearing the intense rains outside, Weatherman reached for his radio and flicked it on.

The same rattling buzz-screech was playing again, this time on loop—which meant that things were getting serious. The automated voice informed us of a tornado warning, and we both knew we could not stay.

Immediately, we began packing up our things. All we had left to do was remove the tarp, pack away the tent, and trek out. I went out to grab my tarp first, as it is an expensive piece of equipment, and we both figured if we had to leave the cheap tent, that'd be okay.

When I had finished with the tarp, I returned to the tent to grab my bag and start planning a way out. I sat down, Weatherman across me, and looked at my map to figure out a route.

SOMETHING WAS MIMICKING THE BUZZ SOUND FROM OUTSIDE OUR TENT.

I was lost in my map and compass when that weather alert buzz-screech played again.

Startled, I said to Weatherman, "Will you please turn that damn thing off? It's a little annoying."

There was no response.

I looked up at Weatherman, who was white as a ghost and looking me dead in the eyes.

"It . . . wasn't . . . me," he stammered, and I knew he wasn't joking around. Soon, the buzz happened again. We sat silent, and the buzz came again and again, more and more unnerving each time.

Something was mimicking the buzz sound from outside our tent.

We both tried to be as quiet as we could and continued to sit in silence.

Suddenly, there was a buzz that was louder than ever, obviously coming from right outside our tent. It was loud enough to make my ears ring and to suppress the screaming from Weatherman's agape mouth. Without a word, we burst out of the tent, into the blinding rain, and toward the nearest road. We sprinted in the direction of the truck and didn't stop until we were inside, on our way home.

When I returned to the site about three days later to recover the tent, to my surprise, it was still in excellent condition. The door, still open from our sudden departure, revealed the only thing inside: Weatherman's radio, smashed to pieces.

To this day, Weatherman shivers like a leaf when he hears that buzzing sound on the radio. Neither of us has stayed the night at the park since—but I may return soon.

Beware of strange weather in Cuyahoga Valley or in the forest at all. There's no telling what hides in the cloak of rain, waiting for thunder to strike to mask its own.

DID I SEE A ZOMBIE BIGFOOT?

While we imagine all sorts of monsters, we rarely think about the afflictions they might have. These conditions may convert something that is already frightening into an entirely different kind of nightmare.

FIELD NOTES

Location: Pacific Northwest, USA
Date/Time: An early autumn afternoon
Atmosphere: Stinky . . . with a hint of decay

I used to be a game warden for a certain state I don't want to name. I'd seen a lot of weird stuff in my eight years there before a drunk poacher injured me in a gunfight. One of the stranger things I'd ever seen during my employment was something I saw walking past my vicinity one early autumn afternoon.

Dispatch received a call about a person shooting at some deer right outside of someone's home from the street, and that the person shooting was inside a blue truck parked on the shoulder of the road—which is very illegal. So, I headed to the location and met up with another game warden, and we started investigating the site. The shooting occurred directly beside a spacious house with a sizable lawn that seamlessly blended into a densely forested area.

My coworker and I came across a .30-06 shell casing, the distinct smell of gunpowder lingering in the air. While my partner interviewed the eyewitness—who heard the shot and peeked out the window in time to see the blue truck drive off—I searched the area for a possible bullet impact or even blood drops from a wounded animal.

I THOUGHT IT WAS THE WOUNDED DEER AND WAS ABOUT TO STEP FORWARD TO GET SIGHT OF IT WHEN A REPUGNANT ODOR REACHED MY NOSE.

I eventually made my way to the tree line, where I lucked out and found a fresh impact spot on a tree. I took stills of it with my phone, and then I noticed that there was a bit of blood on the ground off to the side. I followed it into the woods. The land flowed up onto a steep but short ridge covered in trees, and beyond was some type of narrow gully that looked like it flooded during heavy rains.

I stopped on top of this ridge line and looked around, having lost the sparse blood trail. I scanned my surroundings slowly. That was about the time I started hearing something moving through the forest. It was coming from up the gully on my right, but out of sight because of all the trees. I thought it was the wounded deer and was about to step forward to get sight of it when a repugnant odor reached my nose.

There was a faint scent of decaying meat and other smells I won't mention. If you've been near corpses, you know it's not just the decomposing flesh that smells, but also what they'd consumed. And what's worse is that it was getting stronger—and so was this noise. It was like something casually passing through thick bushes and dragging its feet across the ground. Whatever it was, it wasn't trying to be sneaky.

I was just about to call out. "Game warden!" to see if it was a person, but then I caught sight of something in the narrow spaces of the tree trunks. I couldn't move as I caught a flash of something dark brown, or possibly mottled dark and brown, gradually coming closer from the bushy gully.

The smell was much stronger now, and I had to breathe more through my mouth.

I could make out a little more detail through the trees now. I could see flashes of hair or fur, but it was complex, and the moments I could see it between the trees were too short to absorb or process much detail. Eventually, the trees became

Many Bigfoot enthusiasts dedicate their time and effort to researching and investigating reported sightings, footprints, and eyewitness accounts. In an unusual twist, the FBI became involved in the Bigfoot phenomenon. In 1976, the agency received hairs believed to be linked to Bigfoot. The FBI conducted an analysis on the hairs to determine their origin. Disappointingly, the official analysis concluded that the hairs were, in fact, of deer origin.

less dense. I could gradually discern the shape and form of this thing as it passed between the thinning trees.

It was large, very large.

I want to say it was eight feet (2 m) tall with very broad shoulders. It was covered from head to toe in dark brown hair, but there was more to its appearance.

The face looked like a caveman who hadn't shaved once in his life.

One eye was missing, while the other was foggy white.

The mouth was agape, and it looked like it was missing some of its lower lip.

The torso was patchy, with large, deep gashes. Its dark leatherlike skin barely covered the gray muscle tissue underneath. But the worst part was that its abdomen was mostly missing, and what intestines remained were dangling off its right hip. Its left thigh had a huge part missing on the outside, and its right foot was completely absent. It was stepping on its own ankle stump.

I was frozen. I don't think I even breathed for the whole time.

It sort of lazily meandered past my eyes, down the gully. I eventually lost sight of it and the smell was fading. I quietly returned to my partner, who was extracting the bullet.

He could tell I'd seen something weird because of the look on my face and just nodded and said, "Had a jump out in the woods?" That's our local lingo for "Did you see something weird out there?"

I just nodded and headed to my patrol truck and downed an entire bottle of water from a cooler.

To this day, I have no clue where it was going, where it came from, or how it got that way. I can only truly hope that it is an extremely rare phenomenon and we all won't have to worry about it on a bigger scale.

There is a type of disease out there that affects deer, elk, and even moose called CWD, or Chronic Wasting Disease. It's very nasty, and I've had to put down deer who had it. But whatever the Bigfoot I saw that night had, that was not it. This creature was very dead. Its flesh and soft tissue were gray toned.

I really think what I saw was a Zombie Bigfoot.

A TERRIFYING ENCOUNTER IN SMALL-TOWN OHIO

What should be a routine call warps as the sun goes down. It doesn't matter whether you believe in monsters. There's one waiting for you in the woods.

FIELD NOTES

Location: Defiance, Ohio, USA
Date/Time: A dark night in the 1980s
Atmosphere: Gloomy and uncertain, surrounded by trees

Back in the '80s, my dad had a friend named Joe. He told my dad about this encounter, and then my dad told me.

Joe worked for the Ohio Parks and Wildlife Division. He usually worked in the Columbus area, but on this occasion, he was in a town called Defiance—where the Independence Dam State Park is located.

Joe described the park as being well-hidden, nestled between a wide river and a thick forest of tall trees. Once inside, it was long and narrow, with a small camping area in the back. There was only one way in and one way out, with dense forest surrounding it. What follows is the encounter Joe had as told through his perspective.

Joe met with the sheriff, David, at his office. The day was uneventful until around 9 p.m., when a call came in requesting the sheriff and Joe respond to a couple camping out at the Dam. After about a fifteen-minute drive, they arrived at the very last campsite, where an older silver RV was sitting.

There they saw a couple in their forties, a man and a woman, waiting outside. The sheriff addressed the couple while Joe began looking around. The first thing that caught Joe's attention was the disarray of everything. The lawn chairs were overturned or damaged, the picnic table was completely destroyed, and the heavy-duty grill—mounted on a concrete slab—was folded in half.

The couple said they had arrived earlier in the day to set everything up and get ready for a relaxing weekend of camping. They had gotten the feeling they were being watched and went to catch fish to shake the sensation. While doing so, they noticed nature had gone silent, and it pushed them further into unease. No birds singing, crickets chirping, nothing. They chose to play it safe and returned empty-handed.

The couple returned to their RV and started preparing dinner when it started shaking violently, causing them to fall to the floor. It sounded as if something surrounded them on each side of the RV, but they didn't hear or see anything. After several minutes of being tossed around like rag dolls, the husband shouted he had a gun.

The rocking abruptly stopped, and they could feel long, low bellows vibrating beneath their feet. Remember, this was the '80s, so they didn't have cell phones to call for help. They waited for a while before grabbing their gun, throwing the RV door open, and rushing to their truck. They drove to a payphone and called for help.

The sheriff reassured the couple, telling them they would check the area and find the people responsible. Joe said he would never forget what the lady said next.

"You aren't looking for 'people,' sheriff . . . you're looking for monsters."

David went back to his vehicle, grabbed a shotgun, tossed a flashlight to Joe, and they headed into the woods.

Joe didn't for a moment think it was anything other than a bunch of teenagers, but he noticed a look of concern on David's face. The deeper they went, the darker it got. It became so dark that Joe could only see a couple of feet in front of him.

At one point, he realized that David had stopped walking. When he turned to say something, he was met with a quick "shh" as he watched David point his finger

According to the legend, Lycaon was the king of Arcadia and a descendant of Zeus. However, Lycaon was notorious for his wickedness and arrogance. To test the omniscience of the gods, he decided to serve them a gruesome feast. Lycaon killed his own son and cooked him, mixing the flesh with that of an animal. He then served this abhorrent meal to Zeus himself. Enraged by this act of sacrilege, Zeus transformed Lycaon into a wolf as punishment. Thus, Lycaon became the first werewolf in Greek mythology, forever cursed to roam the earth in the form of a savage beast. The legend of Lycaon serves as a cautionary tale, warning against disrespecting the gods and the consequences that may follow.

toward the darkness. Joe shined the flashlight where he was pointing, about fifteen feet (5 m) away. The flashlight weakly penetrated the thick foliage and dense trees.

"Between the trees," David whispered.

Joe started cautiously walking forward, moving the flashlight slowly up and down when he saw something.

Pressed up against a tree was a leg—a man's leg, but bigger and hairier.

He then saw a long, oddly shaped hand that reminded him of what a human hand might look like if it had been broken and never healed properly. Instead of nails, it had claws that were long, sharp, and wide.

Joe felt his heart drop into his stomach as his legs weakened. Then he felt it—the vibration beneath his feet that the couple had described, followed by long, deep growls. The air filled with a suffocating, pungent odor, causing both men to recoil in disgust. Joe moved the flashlight up about eight feet (2 m) off the ground when he saw a face.

It was covered in thick, brownish-gray hair and had the muzzle and teeth of a large canine. The eyes looked like two dancing orange flames—and they were looking right at them.

"Shoot it," Joe whispered to David. As soon as those words left his mouth, several of these creatures began creeping out from behind the trees.

YOU AREN'T LOOKING FOR "PEOPLE," SHERIFF... YOU'RE LOOKING FOR MONSTERS.

"We gotta get out of here," David muttered while slowly walking backward. Joe was the most terrified he had ever been in his life and couldn't get his legs to move. He couldn't see them, but he could feel them closing in with every passing second.

The vibrations had become painful by this point, making him feel as if his spine were about to explode. Joe feared mysterious predators would kill him.

Out of nowhere, there was a brilliant flash that lit up the surroundings, accompanied by a thunderous crash.

Terrifying screams filled the air. Joe ran for his life. Afterward, he learned that David had witnessed movement behind him and discharged the shotgun in that direction to scare away whatever those things were.

Eventually, they made it back to the campers. Both men were bruised shades of black and blue, with scratches from head to toe from running blindly. The sheriff immediately made them vacate the area. They closed the park for a few weeks after that incident, telling the public it was for "repairs." Before Joe left to come back home, he asked the sheriff what he thought they saw that night.

Without hesitation, he said, "A werewolf."

He then told him about the Defiance Werewolf spotted back in the '70s. Apparently, a railway worker had an encounter with one stalking the tracks late one night.

Even many, many years later, Joe says it's one of the most vivid memories he has.

He'll never understand the mysterious vibrations or their cause, but he knows they were real. He'll never go back to that part of Ohio.

MORBID MOUNTAINS

As you climb, the air thins, and the temperature drops. Your body betrays you, taking in less oxygen. Headaches, vomiting, dizziness. When you set up camp, attempting to wrest away the symptoms of altitude sickness, you find yourself sleepless.

The noises outside keep you awake. Neither birds, nor insects. Instead, a harrowing crunch of footsteps. You hold your breath, realizing that whatever is walking around out there is trying to sneak around. It's getting closer, still hiding its presence.

Not yet.

The mountains are beautiful. Snowy peaks and lush greenery. It can be tempting to crave a hike into those wondrous altitudes. But make no mistake, the beauty of nature conceals its most peculiar terrors. For what might hide itself away in the mountains save for those things from which mankind escaped? The cold. The pressure.

The monsters.

A GOBLIN CREATURE ATTACKED MY DOG

Many have echoed the belief that animals possess a heightened sensitivity to the supernatural. We seldom ponder the actions we would take if our beloved pets were thrust into a fight for their lives against an unknown creature.

FIELD NOTES

Location: Outside the Banana Cave, UK
Date/Time: Time to take the dogs for a walk
Atmosphere: Like any other normal day, until . . .

This is quite possibly the strangest and most intense encounter I have ever had. Not only did it happen to me, but also to my dog and my friend's dog, too.

In our local woods in the northeast of England, there is a path beside a cliff face—and on those cliffs, there is a series of small caves we call the Banana Cave. I was never sure why, but the cliffs are made of limestone and have a slight yellow tint. Maybe it was the shape of the caves, but that's not important.

Many people—locals, dog walkers like us, birdwatchers—frequently use the path we walked. It's not exactly a quiet path, which is why this was as shocking as it was.

My dog and my friend's dog are great, and they are amazing off their leashes. They just go and do what they do and don't bother anyone or any dogs. Of course, dogs will be dogs. Mine, being a bit of an adventurer, began climbing the bank toward the cliff face and near the caves.

UPON CLOSER INSPECTION, I NOTICED THAT IT HAD A FACE RESEMBLING THAT OF A BAT, COMPLETE WITH TWO MENACING, POINTY FRONT TEETH.

I called him down. More than once. Despite my efforts, I noticed something had caught his eye because his head went low, and his ears went back. I thought it was strange because if it was a rabbit or a squirrel, he'd have chased it. Instead, he was as still as a statue. I shouted louder this time for him to come back down to the path.

Then there was a huge commotion. He went into fight mode, backing up while barking and snapping at whatever the hell it was. I scrambled up the bank myself in a panic. I made sure it wasn't a badger, as they can act erratically when cornered.

My dog charged forward, and that was it. He yelped and barked, and it was awful.

What I saw was a monkey-like creature with pointy ears.

There wasn't any fur that was visible to me. It had a black and leathery appearance, with eyes as dark as midnight. It latched itself onto my dog's neck, hanging onto it like the way a sloth does. My dog shook and rolled, but whatever this thing was, it held on.

Despite running until my heart pounded against my ribcage, it seemed like an eternity before I finally reached my dog.

My friend's dog joined in on the commotion as she ran past me and began barking and snarling at the creature and my dog. As I got closer, I picked up a stick and instantly swung at the little creature, terrified it was seriously hurting my dog. I hit the creature directly on the back of its head.

It didn't budge straight away, so I hit it again. This time, the stick broke in half when hitting its back.

The creature bounded off my dog, its movements resembling that of a playful monkey. Upon closer inspection, I noticed that it had a face resembling that of a bat, complete with two menacing, pointy front teeth. It spun around and appeared to have lost footing, but eventually dashed off on all fours, climbed up the cliff face, and disappeared over the cliff edge.

Luckily, my dog was pretty much unharmed. He had a slight cut above his eye, a cut on his nose, and a cut on his chest that looked worse than it was—there was just a lot of blood.

I have no idea what this thing was, but my friend saw it from the bottom of the bank and confirmed the exact same thing I saw. I believe it to be some sort of goblin, but beyond that, I have no idea. I'm positive that there is at least one person who has encountered something similar prowling in Northeast England—

Waiting for its next meal.

According to local folklore in northern England, Boggarts were mischievous beings that delighted in causing chaos and tormenting their victims. They were known for pranks, shapeshifting, and creating eerie noises. Superstitious individuals would take precautions to ward off Boggarts, such as placing iron objects near doorways or leaving offerings of milk and honey. Naming a Boggart was dangerous, as it was believed to unleash its full wrath. In the marshlands, it was thought doing so brought madness and accidents. While some dismiss these stories as superstition, belief in Boggarts remains ingrained in the folklore of northern England, with some claiming to have witnessed their presence.

THE CAVE IN THE MOUNTAIN

Humans have long since battled the call of the unknown.
Peering deep into a dark cave, instinct and curiosity edge us forward, daring
us to explore. Despite what, or who, might lurk in the shadows.

FIELD NOTES

Location: The hills of Mexico
Date/Time: Just before sunset
Atmosphere: An unfathomable darkness, unbearably hot

I was around ten years old when I first encountered the cave.

I am the youngest of three to Mexican American parents. In my childhood, I traveled to Mexico at least twice a year. My folks both come from a small village in the desert valley in central Mexico. During my childhood and adolescence, the village, or town, whatever you'd like to call it, had a maximum of three hundred residents. Everybody knew everybody. You get it.

As a child, going from the downtown of a major Texas city to the lawless deserts of Mexico was liberating in a way. I could do whatever I wanted at any time, with little apparent consequence. I discovered a lot about myself and learned to respect life and nature while hunting and working in the hills of Mexico.

A popular pastime for the folks of the town was to hike up the mountain just outside of town. It took all day to reach the top, but when you did, you could enjoy a view of the entire town and the valley while the sun was setting. It was a truly enjoyable experience.

While atop the mountain one evening, my close friend from the village, who accompanied me daily during my visit, revealed the existence of a massive cave on the other side of the mountain.

"I've never been on that side of the mountain. There's a cave back there?" I asked.

It felt odd to me, despite how many times I took a trek to the top of the mountain, that no one had mentioned this cave to me.

"Let's go," he said, not waiting for me to respond.

He got up from the giant boulder we were sitting on and started up over the peak of the mount. I followed right behind him. He had gotten me into some trouble before, but I had never really gotten hurt because of him, so I thought, "Why not?"

There are no trails or markers on the mountain. It took some searching, but eventually we found the cave. It was indeed a giant hole carved into the mountain, going down as far as I could see. The setting sun didn't light up more than a few yards into the tunnel before fading into pure darkness.

We stood at the edge, peering down into the depths of the cave. Almost instantly, my eyes and nose started to feel like I had stuck my face in hot coals. The smell of ammonia from the bats that lived in the cave blindsided me. Meanwhile, my bud was having a good laugh at the expense of my tear ducts and nose hairs.

We stared down into the giant hole for a good minute, looking around at all the bats clinging to various rock formations. I pointed at some beams of wood— or maybe they were really long tree trunks—that were placed across the cave at varying depths.

"What are those for?" I asked.

"Farmers hire people to climb down there and bag bat poop to use as fertilizer. They make a lot of money. Want to take some?" he asked excitedly.

I declined, not wanting to go into the cave at all. But as I expected, my friend had already begun his descent. He made his way down to the first section that had sufficiently flat ground to stand on without the aid of the wooden beams.

He yelled at me to follow him, and I don't quite remember how, but he convinced me to climb down into the cave. Since the beams were placed by and intended for adults, they had a considerable distance between them. My smaller frame slipped through without issue. We both stood on the small section of level ground, trying not to breathe as the smell was burning our lungs.

HOWEVER, AS HE CLIMBED HIGHER UP THE WOODEN BEAMS TOWARD ME, THE DWINDLING SUN ILLUMINATED THE LOOK OF FEAR ON HIS FACE.

"Come on," he said, and continued to the next beam underneath us.

"I'm not going down there, man," I said back to him, my shaky voice bouncing off the surrounding walls.

He didn't stop, though. Although he heard me and possibly assumed I would follow him closely, he continued until the darkness engulfed him. I could hear him whistle at me from unique positions inside the cave. And eventually, I didn't hear him at all.

He had either stopped whistling entirely or he went so deep into the cave that I couldn't hear him anymore. He had mentioned that once it got to a certain depth, the floor evened out and you could easily walk deeper into the cave.

Bats started to fly out in swarms. I knew they wouldn't purposefully hurt me, but they were very loud and distracting. It was a struggle to remain in place as the tide of bats brushed by me. Once most of them passed, and I could, for sure, be heard if I yelled into the cave, I called out to my friend.

"Hey, man, let's go before it gets dark!"

I stood there waiting for a reply, but he never called back to me. I looked around, debating whether I should stay put or climb out and wait for him outside the cave. Tucked into the spaces between the rocks on the walls of the cave, I noticed a few empty rice bags. I assumed they were used for carrying the bat poop.

I also noticed what looked to be clothes snagged on the edges of the rocks on the walls lower into the caves. Shoes were left on the small ledges that naturally occurred in the cave.

"Odd," I thought, thinking some folks found it easier to climb down while barefoot.

I heard huffing coming from beneath me. It was the unmistakable sound of my friend's heavy, panicked breathing. I tried my hardest to see down into the darkness, but it was no use. My friend would frequently play tricks on me, so I hesitated to believe that he was actually in some kind of trouble.

The sounds of panic were getting closer though, and the distress in his breath became apparent.

When he came into view, he had a look that I initially misunderstood as anger, as if he were unhappy that I didn't follow him down. However, as he climbed higher up the wooden beams toward me, the dwindling sun illuminated the look of fear on his face. He didn't stop to let me up first. He passed by me in a hurry and was out of the cave before I even made a move. I looked down once more at the darkness beneath me and saw nothing and heard nothing.

I focused on balancing as I navigated through the beams until I made it out of the cave. Once I was out, I looked around for my friend so we could leave, but I didn't see him anywhere near the mouth of the cave. I yelled for him, getting ready to accept that he had probably left me behind again, and was halfway down the mountain. I called him one more time and scanned around for him until I found him at the tree line, sitting next to a big rock.

"Hey, man, let's go before it gets dark," I said again as I walked toward him. I was so relieved I wouldn't have to find my way down the mountain on my own in the dark. He just sat there, looking bewildered. I was trying to figure out what he was thinking or why he was behaving so weirdly. He started breathing heavier and heavier with each breath, and anger began to settle into his face.

I backed away, knowing what he could do in his rage. He was a good guy who wouldn't hurt me or anyone that wasn't truly asking for it, but while in a blinding rage, he had once knocked his brother, who just happened to be in the line of fire, unconscious. I wasn't in the mood to get floored.

He rose from the ground and made his way toward the cave. While picking up a big rock, he ended up smashing his thumb, fueling his anger further. With the rock in his arms, he walked to the opening, lifted it up, and sent it crashing down into the dark hole.

The rock broke through some of the wooden beams on its way down and caused an enormous roar of echoes that filled the surrounding air. When the intense roar of echoes started to subside, my friend looked like he was getting nervous. He gave me a look and nodded toward the trees, telling me it was time to go.

Whenever we hiked up the mountain, we would run down at full speed, jumping from one boulder to another. It was our tradition. The mountain's steep face was covered in decades of dirt and dead leaves, cushioning our landings. Dangerous, yes. But most of the activities we filled our days with were dangerous. We were just kids with only our imaginations to entertain ourselves.

When we started jumping and hopping down the mountain, my friend was covering way more ground than I was. I tried my best to keep up, but he left me behind, seemingly without even trying. He would stop now and then to let me catch up, though. We made it back to town in about forty minutes.

We sat in my family's living room for a while, which was no more than an open-air concrete corridor with a roof made of bamboo and clay shingles. He held his hand up and showed me his thumb. It was a disgusting purple, swollen lump.

"I need to drain the blood," he said as he blankly stared at his hand. I found him a sewing needle and held it over a candle for a few seconds. I slowly pierced the skin of his thumb with the needle, and I could see it hurt him quite a bit.

He was really quiet after that.

Bodies are often found in caves, whether they are victims or criminals. Bodies like Joseph Henry Loveless', who was a notorious criminal and bootlegger active in the early twentieth century. His disappearance in 1916 remained a mystery until his remains were discovered in the Civil Defense caves, in Idaho, USA, decades later. His dismembered and headless body was found in two separate instances in 1979 and 1991. Despite the gruesome state, his remains were well-preserved, allowing investigators to identify him. The circumstances and motive behind his brutal murder remain intriguing, making this case one of the most perplexing in Idaho's history.

BUT EVERY YEAR I VISITED AFTER THAT, HE WAS NEVER THE GUY I KNEW AS A KID.

Maybe it was that we turned into teenagers soon after. But every year I visited after that, he was never the guy I knew as a kid.

In 2020, during the summer, I received news that my good friend was discovered, hanged, in his room at his house. I have no doubt that he had enemies in town and in the surrounding villages who might have had something to do with his death. However, his wife said she was sure he had hanged himself.

He was there with me when I went on my first hunt, when I harvested my first beehive, when I unknowingly stole a herd of cattle from the drug lord in our region, when we got lost in the desert and jumped into a well just to drink water, when my aunt unloaded her rifle on us when she thought we were trespassers, and when we were chased by a herd of bulls that got away from their rancher.

I often wonder what happened in that cave that really changed him. I really regret not being there with him that day.

Chaneques come to us from Aztec folklore. They are believed to be small, spritelike beings who serve as elemental forces and guardians of nature. These ethereal creatures are usually petite in stature and are often seen without clothing. They prefer inhabiting forests, rivers, or caves and possess a profound spiritual affinity for the earth and water.

According to legends, the Chaneque's attacks are so terrifying that they can cause a person's soul to flee their body. Without completing a specific ritual to retrieve their soul, the victim's health rapidly declines, and they meet their demise.

A CRYPTID NEAR MT. ADAMS

Surrounded by cliffs, the absence of sound from heavy machines amplifies the feeling of solitude, making you question the wisdom of venturing so far. Because you are isolated, but not alone.

FIELD NOTES

Location: Old Maid's Canyon, Oregon, USA
Date/Time: The tail end of a hard day's work
Atmosphere: Foul air; the uncertainty of unknown intentions

In 2003, I had been working for a gravel company off and on for about one to two years. In my first year, I was shoveling gravel under a rock crusher and clearing the belts for the crushing machine. It was the dirtiest job I'd ever had, but it built character and humbled me deeply.

The following year, around late summer or early fall, my boss got a job up in the mountains on my rez. We were crushing rock and layering it over the back roads for logging trucks, timber being one of the main moneymakers for my tribe—aside from the Indian Casino, a.k.a. Legends Casino.

But back to the job. We started in Old Maid's Canyon, which is a valley located in Oregon. I had my shovel ready, but my boss told me to come with him and set the shovel down. They promoted me to roller operator.

Not only was I no longer working the dirtiest job I had ever worked, but my boss gave me a $2 raise for running the roller. By the second day operating the roller, I was on my own, but stuck close to the rock crusher and trucks to get more familiar with the roller.

By the third week on the job, I had gained confidence with the machine. We were paving farther and farther away from the crushing site. So, the intervals between seeing the trucks that dump the asphalt grew long. Deep into Old Maid's Canyon, a truck passed me and dumped the gravel. The backhoe came in and leveled it out, and now it was my turn to pack it down with the roller. I had a CD Walkman to listen to music and drown out the noisy roller.

I had the vibration turned on and put the roller into gear to move forward. The truck and backhoe were gone. With my headphones on and treating this like any other day of work, I was at least five, maybe six miles (8 to 10 km) away from the crushing site. The roller runs slow regardless, so I can't necessarily kick the sucker into fifth gear and run out of there in a hurry.

I found myself in an area where the canyon and tree line bordered the road I was rolling on. The wind had picked up and blew in my direction. I smelled the stench of something that seemed like rotted meat and seven-year-old body odor. It literally made me want to vomit. I figured maybe a dead deer or elk was nearby.

I looked all around me and realized just how enclosed this area was with the canyon and trees surrounding me. To the left was a cliffside slightly hidden by tall tamarack trees, but I could see rock from the cliffside through them. I took my headphones off, pulled the roller over, and shut it off. The smell had become so strong; I knew I had to be close to the dead animal or whatever was near the road.

I heard rocks falling from the cliffs to the left and I looked over there since it caught my attention. There was grunting, deep and muffled, as if someone or something was trying to be quiet while running uphill on the cliffs. I gazed through the trees; the wind picked up again, blowing the stench once more toward me.

Through the branches, I caught sight of the thing.

It had fur unlike anything I had ever seen in my entire life! The fur and body attached to it was orange brown in the sunlight and covered a very muscular back.

People have told me I probably just saw a bear. My stepdad at the time, who landed this job for me and drove a truck for this company, even said it was a bear. But I know what I saw after spending years on my rez. Many people on my rez had spotted Spil'yay and Bigfoot, and I had heard stories about them growing up.

IT WAS LIKE IF BIGFOOT AND A DOGMAN SPLICED THEIR GENES AND CREATED AN ANIMAL IN THEIR IMAGE.

This thing grunted and whooped once it reached the top. I saw a good portion of what it was. To my amazement and anxiety, it looked like an ape—bipedal.

The face had the same orange and brown fur covering it, and a snout that protruded like a dog's.

It was like if Bigfoot and a Dogman spliced their genes and created an animal in their image. The body of the Bigfoot had to have been eight to nine feet (2 to 3 m) tall. Its eyes were a sharp yellow and almost glowed, even though it was daylight. It ran away and out of sight. What happened in merely a few minutes had left a huge impact on me.

Realizing I was alone and miles away from people and the crusher, I put the roller in reverse, backed the thing up, and started my way back to the crushing site. The smell was gone; everything seemed to return to as it was before.

Before it happened, I didn't realize no birds, owls, or anything were around. They would usually fly past me and chirp along the trees into their nests. I noticed this wasn't happening at all. No one believed what I saw. I tried to tell my coworkers and my now ex-stepdad.

I never ventured far from the trucks after that. If I ended up alone, my stepdad left me with a pistol to keep on me just in case I came across a "bear" again. I think the reason people didn't want to believe me was because they didn't want to fear anything while working so deep in the mountains near Mt. Adams.

I believe I saw a trickster or Spil'yay, and it scared me to the point that I couldn't wait for this job in the mountains to be over. Once we laid gravel on all the logging roads, I never returned to this job. My mom and stepdad ended up divorcing not long after. I was twenty-four years old.

The only person who believed me was my mom. Her brother had seen Sasquatch when he was young. My uncle, Creator bless his soul, died tragically in a car accident when I was nine, and I never got to hear his story. But he claimed he saw Bigfoot. Our mountains have creatures residing in them: Bigfoot, Spil'yay, UFO sightings.

I believe Spil'yay spared me that day. Instead of messing with me, it scurried away and grunted once at the top of the cliffs, as if to say, "You're lucky I'm letting you go," before disappearing over the top of the cliffside. I bet creatures exist all over the world that we can't begin to comprehend, hiding in places similar to where I saw Spil'yay.

But as a Native American myself, I believe that coexisting with things, even if we don't completely understand them, is a part of life. I'm just thankful that I was able to survive my encounter so I could be around to tell this story.

The Yakama, a federally recognized Native American tribe with over ten thousand members, have a rich folklore that is steeped in legends and mythical creatures. One prominent figure in their tales is Spil'yay (pronounced "speeli-eye"), the legendary trickster, often disguised as a coyote, that used daring and humor to teach mankind about survival and living in harmony with nature.

BIGFOOT IS A SHAPESHIFTER

In our homes, nothing is supposed to reach us. The dangers are supposed to loom outside. Even so, they can still observe us, imprinting fear in the external world.

FIELD NOTES

Location: The mountains of West Virginia, USA
Date/Time: One productive night
Atmosphere: Cozy, working on crafts with YouTube videos playing in the background

This happened to me on a mountain in West Virginia where I live. Only three households live up there, all of us retired, and among us, we own just over twenty acres (8 ha). Our property is next to the Summit, a 10,600-acre (4,290 ha) Boy Scouts' property, which is next to over seventy thousand acres (28,328 ha) of preserved wilderness. Naturally, there is a lot of wildlife in this area. My husband has chickens, and because he likes to keep tabs on what might mess with them, he keeps a trail cam posted near the coop.

We see raccoons, foxes, one bobcat, one mountain lion (the Department of Natural Resources will tell you West Virginia doesn't have them, but we do), a lot of coyotes, and every so often a bear.

The layout of the property is important.

The three households own a lot of land. Our homes are situated in a triangular pattern. At the top left of the triangle, the neighbor's house is set far back from the gate entrance, and it's always dark at night. The neighbor at the top right and up a slight hill has a dusk-to-dawn light, and we, at the bottom point of the triangle, have motion lights

When we built our house, we had an attached garage, but later my husband decided we needed a three-car garage behind the house. He's a retired carpenter and gets

Do you know where the legend of Bigfoot began? In 1958, journalist Andrew Genzoli of *The Humboldt Times* published a letter from a reader about loggers in Northern California who had discovered large footprints. Genzoli jokingly referred to the possibility of a relative of the Abominable Snowman and found that the story fascinated readers. In response, Genzoli and fellow journalist Betty Allen published follow-up articles, giving the creature the name "Big Foot." And thus marked the beginnings of a legend.

bored, so he invents things to build. I took full advantage of this and turned the attached garage into my crafts room.

One night, I was sitting in my crafts room doing my thing. I like to listen to YouTube videos while I work, so I was picking out a playlist on my iPad. It was about 10:30 p.m., very dark outside, and I had the garage door up because it was warm.

The only light I could see was from my garage and a small amount of my neighbor's dusk-to-dawn light, which only dimly lit up a section of the driveway.

My nine-year-old beagle was sleeping on the floor next to me when he started to growl. We've had him since he was six weeks old, so I've heard him growl before—but never like this. I looked down at him and then in the direction he was looking. It was standing in the middle of my neighbor's drive about halfway up the hill.

I instantly knew that it wasn't human.

It was, I guess, about seven-and-a-half feet (2 m) tall, maybe. The thing was standing on two legs, and because of the dim light, I couldn't tell if it was facing me or the other direction. I know bears will stand up; I've never seen one do that myself, but I know they do.

The thing didn't look like a bear to me. It was bulky, but not fatty like a bear. When I stood up, it moved. It didn't run; instead, its walk was swift. It walked similar to how a human would, but I knew it wasn't human.

I stood frozen and focused my eyes on the area it went into: the wooded area between the two points of the triangle, between my neighbors' drives. I don't think its fur was black; I got the impression it was dark brown.

I INSTANTLY KNEW THAT IT WASN'T HUMAN.

Once my eyes adjusted, I could see a shadowy shape in the wooded area, and then its color got brighter. And for one split second—I mean if I had blinked, I would have missed it—I saw the shape of its head and shoulder area change.

It wasn't like *An American Werewolf in London*, slow and painful looking, but it happened extremely fast.

It fell down and moments later, the largest coyote I've ever seen emerged, stared at me, and then walked away into the left woods.

I know if a coyote had been in that patch of woods, it would have run out when that thing ran in there. I also know that I saw that thing transform. Shapeshifters were never something I believed in. As far as Bigfoot, I never had an opinion; I liked to believe in him, but didn't ever expect to see one. I don't drink or do drugs.

There is no doubt in my mind about what I saw, even if I struggle to understand. I had my husband check his trail cam, but the thing didn't come near it. If only it had.

CHILDHOOD TRAUMA

A child sits before a TV, wide eyes glued to the screen as John Carpenter's 1982 movie, *The Thing,* plays, watching the scene where Norris' torso implodes into a monstrous mouth which tears Copper's arms clean off. That child was yours truly, back when I was around ten years old. Parents can be too trusting with the "close your eyes" solution. You better believe I peeked through my fingers and saw the most disturbing practical effects imaginable.

Childhood leaves lasting impressions, both positive and negative. Think about the scariest movie scenes and what do you visualize? It's likely a scene from a movie you shouldn't have watched as a kid. The most emotional memories from your youth will stick around for quite some time, for better or worse.

Worse yet, you're never more vulnerable and trusting than when you were young. The bogeyman inhabits the cluttered undersides of children's beds for good reason.

Children are helpless prey.

The stories in this section are about childhood, feeling powerless, and nightmarish encounters that leave lasting memories. These tales are a reminder to keep a protective eye on your children. There's no telling who or what may watch them, too.

THE ANIMAL SKINNER

Animals getting hurt is nothing new. Yet, when a community encounters an act of cruelty against a local pet, it is impossible to overlook. None of them could have anticipated a culprit like this.

FIELD NOTES

Location: A trailer park in Kentucky, USA
Date/Time: During a visit to Mom's new boyfriend
Atmosphere: An injection of shock right into your veins

I am a twenty-nine-year-old woman residing in a comparatively small town in Kentucky. Growing up, my mother sometimes had the most random boyfriends. It was while she was dating a guy who lived in a trailer park that these experiences happened to me. I was about nine years old at the time.

The first experience came about one day when my mom took me and two of my brothers to go visit her boyfriend. The trailer park he lived in was fairly large and surrounded by huge wooded areas.

Many people inhabited the place, and one of them had a small poodle breed dog that frolicked with everyone and craved our attention. His name was Snoopy. Well, one day, Snoopy went missing. He never showed up, and that wasn't normal for him. His owner said he never came home, so a bunch of us got together and began searching for him.

We couldn't find him anywhere, and we searched for hours. We'd pretty much given up hope when someone yelled out that they had found something. I remember sprinting toward a commotion as a crowd formed around a tree in my mom's boyfriend's backyard. My mom tried keeping us kids back, but it was too late.

I saw what it was people were freaking out over. It was a pile of skin and fur. The fur, dirty white, and curly like Snoopy's, remained attached to the skin while the rest of the body was nowhere to be found. We all stared at it in shock, wondering how this could have happened. As far as we knew, no one would have wanted to hurt the little dog. He was a sweet little thing and never bothered anyone except to play. No explanation was really given, and they disposed of the pile of skin and fur.

A couple of weeks later, my mom wanted to go see her boyfriend again. Once again, she took me and two of my brothers along, but first, we stopped by a friend's house who lived in the same trailer park for just a few minutes. When we pulled up and got out of the car, I noticed a little black cat. I love animals, so I went over to pet it before going into the friend's house. We were in there for around ten or fifteen minutes and then left.

While walking back to the car, something caught my eye. Something glistened under the streetlight. It was nighttime, so it was on. I approached it out of curiosity and was surprised to find the body of a small cat. It was the same size as the cat I had just pet only minutes before.

The only issue was that the body had no skin. None whatsoever. It was bone, meat, and muscle, but no skin or fur. It was still wet and emitted some warmth as if it were fresh. I pointed it out to my mom. It grossed her out, but she didn't really make anything of it and told me to leave it alone and get in the car. Snoopy came to my mind, though. I thought it odd that now two animals had been skinned with no explanation.

As the days passed, I put the animals in the back of my mind. We kept visiting my mom's boyfriend and hanging out with the neighborhood kids. And while other odd things would pop up, for me, the scariest thing happened one afternoon when my little brother and I were lying outside on a picnic table in the backyard of my mom's boyfriend's trailer.

As we lay there, my little brother decided to take a nap. I wasn't really sleepy, so I just looked at the clouds and surveyed the surrounding area. The backyard was quite large. There was a vast area of woods back there and a huge field that belonged to a neighbor. Only a thin, rusted wire fence separated the field from the backyard.

IT WAS A PILE OF SKIN AND FUR. THE FUR, DIRTY WHITE, AND CURLY LIKE SNOOPY'S, REMAINED ATTACHED TO THE SKIN WHILE THE REST OF THE BODY WAS NOWHERE TO BE FOUND.

It was in the field that I saw something in the distance. Something that wasn't there before. A figure, standing. At first glance, I thought it was a man. It didn't move at first. But then it seemed to notice me watching and it moved forward. I noticed it had an odd posture.

The right shoulder dipped lower than the left, and its gait was unsteady. As it got closer, I saw more details. It was at least six feet (2 m) tall, maybe more, and what I had thought was regular clothing were more like rags from a distance, hanging off the figure. Its arms were longer than a human's should be, and the hands looked bigger and possibly clawed.

I quickly realized that this wasn't a man I was looking at. My eyes widened, and I shook my little brother awake, pointing to the figure and asking, "Do you see that?!"

He looked toward the figure and his eyes also widened. He nodded. I looked back and realized in horror that the thing had gotten even closer.

It had what looked to be nostrils on its face, kind of how it would look if you cut the nose off a human. Its eyes were pitch black.

The sight of its arm extended toward us sent a shiver down our spines.

I looked back at my brother, fear etched on his face, and urgently whispered, "We should run!"

We both leaped off the table, our legs propelling us forward with such velocity that even the Flash would have been impressed. We ran toward the trailer but didn't even make it out of the backyard before that thing let out a scream.

Kentucky is a hub for local folklore and mysterious creatures. Among these is the infamous Pope Lick Monster, a half-man-half-goat entity said to reside near the trestle bridge over Pope Lick Creek. Legend has it that this creature lures unsuspecting victims onto the treacherous railway tracks below.

Adding to the eerie atmosphere are the chilling tales of Gravediggers, terrifying creatures said to roam graveyards in search of hair. These scavengers, often depicted as shadowy figures with a penchant for the macabre, have become a part of Kentucky's dark folklore, adding to the mystique and allure of the state.

It's hard to describe, but it sounded something like a roar mixed with nails on a chalkboard. It was terrifying, and neither of us looked back to see if the thing was any closer.

We bolted inside, and of course, told my mom. But she didn't really react beyond figuring we were just imagining things. Naturally. But we refused to go back outside.

My mom broke up with her boyfriend not long after that, so we never had to go back to that trailer park. I'm glad.

Something tells me that the thing my little brother and I saw was responsible for those skinned animals. Those woods surrounded the entire area of the trailer park, and I figure that is where it lives and how it travels.

I recently asked my brother if he remembers that night, and his response was, "I sure do. What the hell even was that thing?"

We talked about a few theories but still aren't really sure. All I know is, I'm glad we ran. There's no telling what could have happened had we stayed on that table and the creature caught up to us.

LATE-NIGHT VISIT

We've all stayed up past our bedtime, listening for our parents to avoid their wrath. But when the footsteps approach and the doorknob rattles, how can we be so sure it's them on the other side?

FIELD NOTES

Location: Family home, Chicago, USA
Date/Time: Visiting for Thanksgiving
Atmosphere: Waiting in anxious horror for something that might never appear

I was born and raised in Chicago—in the actual city and not some suburb close by. It was there, in the crowded city, that I learned ghost stories don't only occur in abandoned mansions and rickety shacks.

I live with my parents; they own a multi-family home, and we live on the top floor. My dad bought the house in the early '90s, and it's been in the family ever since. We've never lived anywhere else, and we certainly never plan on leaving; it's a great house in a pleasant neighborhood.

I love this house, and besides minor details about showing its age, I wouldn't change much. That being said, the house has always had a somewhat unsettling vibe. The vibe's not always there, but at certain times of the year, you can feel it more than others, especially at night.

Growing up, I remember experiencing creepy things in the house. Like seeing shadow figures make their way across the hall when I was playing. Hearing footsteps walk from the kitchen to the dining room.

Or hearing the shuffling of things being moved around.

My parents were skeptical if I ever brought it up. Even when things like this happened to them, they brushed it off with a shrug and said something along the lines of, "It's an old house, it creaks."

I never truly believed that.

I always had a rule for myself: never stay in the living room past 1 a.m. And if I ever did because of homework, all the lights had to be on. Despite this rule, whenever I was by myself in the living room, I felt uneasy. The presence in the room was almost tangible, and it gave me shivers down my spine. The best thing I could do was play my music and ignore it. I was always practically running to my room once I was done.

Some people might think it was all in my head, that I was just afraid of the dark or something, but it wasn't. When I left for college, that feeling of something watching me was never there in my dorm room or in my apartment when I eventually began to rent. It was only ever there when I was in my parents' home.

It wasn't until what happened when I came from college for Thanksgiving that my mom finally believed something was off in the house. Everything was fine until the third night of my stay. I had the habit of staying up late at night watching Netflix and that night was no different.

Normally, I never closed my door; I kept it slightly open to let the room "breathe." On this night, though, I closed the door and locked it. My parents had done the same; they always did. It was some time around two or three in the morning that I heard my parents' doorknob jiggle. My parents still had one of the old doors that came with the house, and the doorknob was made of heavy glass.

Because it was an old door with a heavy knob, it would creak loudly when opened and closed. It was practically impossible to make the door quieter. As soon as I heard the all-too-familiar sound of the glass knob turning, my heart sank. I instantly knew that I was about to face some serious trouble.

"Crap," I thought. My mom was probably coming here to yell at me to go to bed. It wouldn't be the first time she'd done it. So, being my sneaky self, I quickly powered off the TV, hid the remote underneath my pillow, wrapped the blanket around myself, and pretended to be asleep.

I remained silent, hearing the footsteps get closer until stopping right outside my door. The doorknob turned slowly; the door jerked—but it was locked, so it didn't budge. I expected my mom to use her fingernail to turn the lock; it wasn't hard to do, but it never happened.

It felt like forever as I waited, and the room had become dead silent.

Suddenly, I got a weird feeling in the pit of my stomach. I slowly looked at the door, focusing my hearing on any noise outside, listening for the footsteps that my mom should've made. Nothing happened. I couldn't hear anything. I became aware of how on edge my nerves had become, and there was no way in hell that I would check it out. So, I forced myself to sleep and wrapped the blanket tighter.

The following morning, I woke up and heard shuffling in the kitchen. I knew it was Mom, so I quickly jumped out of bed and made my way over to where she was. Before I could even get a word out, she said, "What did you want last night?"

I looked at her, confused. "What?"

"You came to my door last night trying to open it. I kept calling out your name, asking you what you wanted, but you never responded. Were you sick or something?" she confidently replied.

"No, no, you came to my door last night. I didn't go to yours," I countered, letting a nervous laugh slip through a weak smile.

"Sam, stop messing with me."

"Mom, I'm not! I thought you were coming to yell at me to go to sleep for being up so late. You turned the knob, but the door was locked, so you couldn't get in."

"I did no such thing," my mom said.

"And neither did I." We just stood there, looking at one another as if trying to

I REMAINED SILENT, HEARING THE FOOTSTEPS GET CLOSER UNTIL STOPPING RIGHT OUTSIDE MY DOOR.

We have whispered ghost stories for generations. Have you ever wondered how many generations? Who was the first to lay eyes on a specter from the afterlife? Well, as far as we know, the world's oldest drawing of a ghost has been found in the British Museum.

On a 3,500-year-old Babylonian clay tablet, a drawing shows a bearded spirit being guided to the afterlife by a companion. The tablet is part of an exorcist's guide for getting rid of unwanted ghosts, specifically addressing the ghost's need for companionship. The ghost is shown with his arms outstretched and his wrists tied by a rope held by the female figure. A text accompanying the drawing describes a ritual that would send them happily back to the underworld.

see who would confess, but neither of us cracked. I obviously knew I didn't get up to go to their room, and I believed that my mom didn't leave her room.

"So, you're not lying to me? Because you like to scare me sometimes." My mom was looking a little more anxious.

"No, Mom, I'm not. If I ever scare you, it's certainly not at two in the morning."

"Okay, then," she said sheepishly. I could tell my mom was now confused and slightly concerned. "Whatever came to visit last night failed. Thank God," she added softly.

I don't know what tried opening both our doors that night, but I was thankful it wasn't able to. I don't know what I would've done if that door had opened. All I know is that something that had been in the house for a long time tried to do something more than just walk around—but it didn't succeed, and I prefer it that way.

THE WEREWOLF OF THE PIG FARM

Farm labor is grueling work. Particularly for someone young and brimming with empathy and curiosity. Unaware of the potential danger, one bad day can attract a hungry predator. And suddenly, you're the one on the chopping block.

FIELD NOTES

Location: Farmland in central Sweden
Date/Time: The turn of the twenty-first century
Atmosphere: A chill in the air, that's thick with smells you'd expect on a farm

The story I'm about to tell happened to me when I was about eleven or twelve years old, so it would have been around the year 2000.

I live in central Sweden. My parents had been divorced for many years; on the day of my encounter, my younger sister and I were visiting our dad at his farm. He was raising slaughter pigs for one of the country's bigger meat producers. I have always loved animals and enjoyed helping at the farm, feeding the animals, and cuddling with the piglets. My dad had built the pig housing just a couple of years before. Let me quickly explain the layout of the building.

When you entered through the main entrance, you'd be at the beginning of a long corridor with four doors on the right side and two more on the left. At the end of the corridor, there was one door leading out to the backside of the building.

The first door on the right led to an office and staffroom, and the second door led to a storage room. The following two doors on the right and the last door on the left led to the three pig stables, which we called stable number one, two, and three. Each stable had forty-eight separate pens where the pigs were housed. The first door on the left went to the barn, where we stored food and straw for the animals.

The farm received pregnant sows a week or two before they were expected to give birth. When the piglets reached an appropriate age, the farm transferred the sows to other farms for a few months of rest before impregnating them again. The piglets stayed with us until they were old enough to be sent for slaughter.

The day of my encounter was a frigid winter day, probably in December or January. The ground was covered in a thick layer of snow and the sky was clear. It was a perfect winter day, and my sister and I had arrived at our dad's place around lunchtime. In the afternoon, we were in the stables, helping with the chores. In stable one, we had young slaughter pigs, and in stable two, pregnant sows ready to give birth soon. Stable number three was empty and had just been cleaned and prepared for a new delivery of pregnant sows to arrive within a few days.

I remember my sister being bored that day because the only thing she liked to do was cuddle and play with newborn piglets—which we didn't have. My dad was in the empty stable, working on a broken gate to one of the pens. It had been damaged in the commotion of moving the slaughter pigs housed there.

I had just fed the pigs in stable number two when my dad told me that he had found one of the slaughter pigs injured. It was quite common for them to get injured during their teenage stage of life when they are trying to establish dominance, being too eager and playful. But it was unusual for them to get any serious injuries. Usually, it was just smaller scratches and bite marks.

When he told me that this pig probably had a broken front leg, my heart dropped because I knew there was nothing we could do, and the pig had to be put down to end its misery. I hated it! It didn't happen often, but when it did, I always started to tear up.

I helped my dad find the injured pig and carry it out through the door to the backside of the building. A big round manure tank was out back, mostly underground, with a meter sticking out. We carried the pig to the other side of the tank, and my dad brought a butchery bolt gun, but I refused to stay out there while my dad did what he had to do.

I went back inside and continued feeding the pigs and listening to music, trying to get my mind off what had happened to that poor pig. After a while, my

There is a condition known as hypertrichosis, also referred to as "werewolf syndrome" due to its resemblance to the mythical creature. Hypertrichosis is an extremely rare genetic disorder characterized by excessive hair growth all over the body, including the face, giving individuals a strikingly similar appearance to werewolves. The condition can be present at birth or develop later in life. It affects both males and females, and the severity of hair growth can vary. Although hypertrichosis is not related to lycanthropy or any supernatural phenomenon, its visual similarity has often led to it being associated with werewolves in popular culture.

dad came to tell me he needed to go to his workshop to get some tools to fix the gate that he was working on; he asked if I wanted to stay or go with him.

He kept his machines and equipment in a workshop close to the farm, and he assured me he'd return shortly, so I opted to wait. I helped him carry some tools to his car and then watched him and my sister drive away.

It was mid-afternoon, but it was already dark outside. I was now alone on the farm. But I didn't mind that. We live just south of the Arctic Circle, and in the winter, we only have a few hours of sunlight from the late morning to early afternoon. I was used to these short winter days and the darkness.

The sky was clear and littered with bright stars, and the moon looked bigger, brighter, and more alluring than usual. I went back inside to the staffroom to eat one of the sandwiches my dad had brought for us. After that, I went back to clean out the pens in stable one and two. The stables had slatted floors that the staff could open to scrape down any feces and straw, which would then automatically transport out to the open manure tank on the backside.

Because of the freezing temperature, I first had to go out to the back to start a circulation pump to keep the liquid manure from freezing in the pipes. I went out the back, opened the hatch to the control panel, and started the pump. I closed the hatch and looked across the manure tank at the pig lying there in the snow.

Only the moon and a dim light shining through the windows from the lights inside lit up the area. The snow under the pig's head was now dyed red. I felt a bit relieved that he was no longer in pain.

I went back inside to start cleaning out the pens, and after about half an hour, I had finished the two stables. My dad and my sister were not yet back from the workshop, so I decided to go to the staffroom to have a Coke from the refrigerator and watch some TV until they came back.

We still had some work to do, but I felt I deserved a break—and they would probably be back any minute. After just a few minutes of watching some boring reality show, drinking Coke, and having my second sandwich, I remembered I had left the circulation pump to the manure tank running.

I put down my sandwich and went out to the corridor toward the back door to turn it off. As I stepped out and prepared to open the control panel hatch, I caught sight of something moving near the manure tank.

I looked toward it and immediately my heart stopped, my entire body frozen from fear.

What I saw was something I had never seen before and really hope I never see again!

Over on the other side of the manure tank, there was a massive animal leaning over the carcass of the pig we had left there earlier that day. The animal was facing away from me, so I could only see its back.

Initially, I mistook it for a large brown bear, but it was much bigger and had a tail with long hair similar to that of a golden retriever. The animal was covered in dark gray and black fur with a wide, muscular upper body, and I could see the steam from its breath rising in the cold air.

Suddenly, the animal stood up on its hind legs—and it was towering! I would guess maybe 2.2 to 2.4 meters (7 to 8 ft) tall. It turned its head slightly to the right, nose toward the sky, and opened its mouth to toss a piece of meat down its throat. The head was definitely a wolf's head, but much bigger and darker. It had long, furry ears pointing upwards and a long snout with big canine teeth.

We have both wild wolves and bears living in this area, but this was something else: bigger, stronger. The feeling I got from looking at it was deeply unsettling.

Werewolves in Sweden and Norway are called *varulv*. The Scandinavian varulv has developed its own mythology, although it bears resemblances to the well-known werewolf folklore: a being that possesses both human and werewolf characteristics, including hairiness and sharp teeth. However, the affliction does not occur due to biting or any other form of violence, which sets it apart from other, more traditional werewolf tales. In much of varulv lore, the creature becomes a werewolf voluntarily, with the use of a certain article of clothing, such as a belt.

The animal leaned over the pig carcass again to continue to feast on its meal. I realized it had not yet noticed me standing behind it. The instincts to fight or flee were at war within me. My teeth clenched and feet refused to move. I finally found the strength to walk silently backward inside, closing and locking the door softly. Not wanting the monster to get inside, I sprinted to the front door to lock it.

I walked back to the door to stable number two that had windows facing the back side, where the creature was. I investigated the stable through the window in the door. The windows on the wall were about 2 meters (7 ft) up from the floor. I could only see the steam from its breath rising in the air outside.

Suddenly, some pigs saw me through the door window and started to grunt loudly. Soon, they were all grunting in a chorus, as they always do when they see a person at the door, excited and hoping I was bringing them food again.

I looked back at the windows just in time to see the creature stand up and turn toward the window and the sound of the pigs.

I could only see the top of its head and its ears when it walked up to the window. I quickly sat down on the floor in front of the door and silently started to cry.

I LOOKED TOWARD IT AND IMMEDIATELY MY HEART STOPPED, MY ENTIRE BODY FROZEN FROM FEAR.

I started crawling on the floor back to the staffroom to get to the phone and call my dad. Remember, this was about the year 2000, when a twelve-year-old didn't have their own mobile phone.

I reached the door and realized that there were two big windows in the staffroom that didn't have any curtains or blinds. The thought of going inside and risking being seen by that thing through the window kept me from entering. I sat down in the corner between the doors to the staffroom and the front door and couldn't hold it in anymore. I started crying like never before. I was sure the monster would get inside—and if it did, it would hear me crying and find me.

Suddenly, the handle on the front door violently turned and something tried to push the door open. I screamed and the handle turned again, followed by two loud thuds trying to break the door open.

My heart pounded in my chest. I was sure I was going to die.

When the door handle stopped moving for the second time, I heard hard knocks on the door and my dad's voice calling for me. I rushed up, unlocking and opening the door, telling my dad and sister to hurry inside, locking the door as they did. When I turned to my dad, he saw that I was crying, and he asked what was wrong. I told him the whole story of what I called the werewolf. He looked at me, not saying a word, then looked at my sister.

He looked back at me and asked if I'd finished feeding and cleaning the pens, and I nodded. He nodded back, thoughtfully looking down at the floor for a few seconds, and then back at us, telling us that the rest of the work could wait until tomorrow before walking us to the house. In the evening, he went by himself to give the pigs their evening meal.

From upstairs, my sister and I anxiously watched him walk across the yard, hoping the creature wouldn't attack him. I remember him looking all around him with a flashlight as he walked.

When he came back, I asked if he had seen the dead pig on the backside. He said he had, or what was left of it.

He said it looked like some predator had found it and dragged the rest of it into the forest.

After this incident, my dad was very clear we were not allowed to go outside after dark.

As I got older, I thought a lot about that day and how my dad reacted after I told him what happened, followed by the strict rules about never going outside after dark. Did he know this creature existed and was lurking in the forests surrounding the farm? Had he seen it himself?

My dad passed away from leukemia some years later, before I had a chance to ask him about it, but I'm sure he knew something about the creature that I saw that day.

MY WEIRD CHILDHOOD

You awaken suddenly, looking at the ceiling. You are aware, but your fingers and legs won't move. Trapped in your own body, you can feel someone—or something—watching you, but you can't do anything about it.

FIELD NOTES

Location: A major metropolitan city, anywhere
Date/Time: Just a little past bedtime
Atmosphere: As if seeing something out of the corner of your eye

As someone who grew up in one of the most urban parts of my country and always heard that the woods were the most haunted places, I was quite surprised when I saw and heard as many things as I did.

After all, the other tales of the women in my family who have this almost-sixth sense were always either religious or lived out in the country, far from any city. The mysterious "gift" has a curious habit of passing over a generation in this family's lineage. I've noticed a pattern—individuals with a birthmark on their right cheek possess this gift. Just like my grandma and great-great-grandma.

Now, I had a very nice childhood—the early 2000s feeling of growing up with no worries other than your Tamagotchi dying. I would spend my days with my dad and nights with my mom, since my father worked the night shift and my mom did your usual nine-to-five.

My routine included waking up, spending time with my dad, having lunch, and going to school. Later, my dad would pick up my mom and me and bring us home. Soon after that, he would go to work, come back at 3 a.m. to eat something, and only be home again at around 6 a.m.

I INITIALLY REGRETTED THAT DECISION WHEN THEY ALL LOOKED AT ME AT THE SAME TIME WITH THESE HORRIBLE, HOLLOW EYES. IT WAS THE FIRST TIME I HAD LOOKED AT THEIR FACES.

My only real problem was bedtime. I hated going to sleep alone. I would always wake up during the night and see *them* in the hallway—shadowy figures that kind of resembled my dad. I knew for a fact that it was not him. It was the size; but again, everything looked big to a six-year-old.

There was also this sway to them, how they moved. I couldn't stop thinking that they reminded me of my dad—if he were a dark, shadowy, floating paranormal creature that didn't make any noise and seemed to move fast.

I saw these beings every night. I had heard stories from the other women in my family about our sixth sense, but my young mind didn't realize that these shadows might be a manifestation of this "gift." Instead, I was always paralyzed with fear.

All I could ever do was stare at them, watching their movements. More seemed to appear with every blink. First, it was just one; but as time went by, there were more. I remember counting eight of them at once, all going between the kitchen, living room, dining room, and bathroom in their crazy dance as my stomach turned on itself in fear until I passed out from tiredness, only waking up in the morning.

This went on for about two years until one day, I decided it was enough. I was tired, sad, and angry because school was stressful, and those damned shadows wouldn't even let me sleep. I could deal with the living during the day, but I needed some "me time" at night. So, in my brilliant eight-year-old heart—but not actually so brilliant mind—I mustered up some courage, went to my door frame, and whispered, "Daddy, is it you?"

I initially regretted that decision when they all looked at me at the same time with these horrible, hollow eyes. It was the first time I had looked at their faces.

But once I took it all in, I wasn't so scared. They just looked at me and disappeared, calmly, like fog rolling out of town in the morning. It was . . . peaceful.

I never saw them again. But thinking back on it, I don't believe they meant any harm. Maybe, just maybe, they were as scared of me as I was of them, or they realized someone could see them and decided to move somewhere else—or hide better. But again, they never did any direct harm, and even though I do not understand why they were there, I know that the way they looked at me was way less scary than how some of the living have.

Do not underestimate the unknown and stay cautious. But know that not everything unexplainable out there means to harm you.

The beings in this encounter sound like what's commonly referred to as "shadow people." They typically appear during sleep paralysis.

What's sleep paralysis, you ask? When the brain has a hiccup and cannot wake you properly, you can sometimes dream while awake.

People report not being able to move in bed while shadowy figures loom over them. Some of these figures have red eyes; others have been seen wearing hats (the Hat Man, for example, is its own phenomenon).

Many cultures have their own version. But surely, we cannot blame sleep paralysis for all these figures . . . right?

IT HUNTS ON FALL NIGHTS

When your car crashes into something, the feeling of your
heart sinking is universal. Thoughts race about what could have been hit
while climbing out. A person? A pet? Or something much worse?

FIELD NOTES

Location: The roads of a residential area in your childhood town
Date/Time: Mid-October, many years ago
Atmosphere: Autumn's warmth, with heavy and panicked breathing

Back in my childhood town, it was a big deal when seasons changed from summer
to fall. Where I lived, it was almost always a toasty 100 degrees Fahrenheit (37°C), so
when it finally dropped below 80 degrees Fahrenheit (26°C) in mid-October, it felt like
a miracle. People spent more time outside because they didn't have to worry about the
seething heat. It lifted their moods. I always loved to go out with my friends and play
until dinner. That was, until . . .

It all started when I was eleven. One or two neighborhood dogs would go missing
here and there, but it seemed to only happen in the fall. Everyone knew about this thing
that took the pets, but nobody talked about it. My cat, one of the first victims, even got
into a fight with it at one point, and he barely escaped with his life. He was lucky.

By the time I was fifteen, people wouldn't even leave their kids unattended when
autumn rolled around for fear of that thing. It was a local legend as far as I was
concerned. Too elusive for our paths to cross. At least, until one day, I was driving
home one night after a long shift at work. I was about sixteen and had just gotten
my driver's license.

I THOUGHT I SAW SOMETHING BEHIND ME, SO I CHECKED MY MIRRORS. WHEN I LOOKED BACK, SOMETHING BIG WAS DARTING IN FRONT OF THE CAR.

I was pulling into my neighborhood like I had done many times before. I thought I saw something behind me, so I checked my mirrors. When I looked back, something big was darting in front of the car.

My attempt to brake was in vain, and I felt my car strike the thing.

It flew back a few feet, but immediately got up and kept running. It was all a blur, and I immediately started freaking out.

What if that was one of my neighbors' pets—or even worse, a human? I decided to make things right by attempting to follow it and check for any injuries. I couldn't live with myself thinking I had just severely injured something and may have even contributed to its death. Before I left, though, something in the back of my mind told me to be cautious. I reached into the glove compartment and grabbed a sharp glass breaker.

Leaving the car, I immediately noticed a trail of blood on the pavement. My face tightened up as I thought I really hurt that thing. I stepped down into the brush. I was surrounded by tall, lush bushes and plants, their leaves brushing against me as I fumbled with my phone's feeble flashlight. It was barely able to pierce through the thick darkness. I walked for a minute or two until I heard a little kid crying. I started freaking out, believing I hit a kid.

Smaller towns seem to be easy pickings for cryptid activity.

If I didn't help the kid quickly, I could be in big trouble. I picked up my pace when suddenly, out of the brush from the direction where I heard the crying, something jumped out. It tackled me to the floor. I dropped my phone. It was snarling and grabbing at me with the intent to kill. This thing wasn't small, either; it was like I was fighting another teenager.

I kicked it off and reached for my pocket and firmly gripped the glass breaker.

It lunged at me again, but this time, I stabbed it right in the middle of its chest. It started to freak out, letting loose these horrendous screams as it darted off into the darkness. I ran back to my car as fast as possible and drove home faster than ever before. It covered me with scratches and blood, but nothing lethal.

I told my parents what had happened, and of course, they didn't believe me. My parents had me take a concussion test the following morning, but it showed that I was mentally healthy. That didn't matter though, because nobody believed me.

At a certain point, I just stopped telling the story. All I have to say is that no more pets or people went missing after that. I escaped with my life, but even more than that, I may have saved a few more lives along the way.

The Enfield Monster sightings in 1973 in Illinois, USA, generated significant attention and media coverage. Eyewitnesses described a grotesque creature standing four to five feet (1 m) tall, with a muscular build and three powerful legs. It had rough, scaly gray skin and piercing red eyes. The creature allegedly struck some individuals, causing scratches and bruises. Despite efforts to track it down, the Enfield Monster disappeared without a trace, leaving the community perplexed. The mystery surrounding its true nature and origin remains unsolved, leading to speculation and intrigue.

CABINS, TENTS, AND CAMPERS

Endless trees, shimmering lakes teeming with fish, starry night skies far from city lights. Such a setting is dreamlike. After weeks of stress and chaos, booking a cabin or planning a camping trip can be tempting.

But when the screaming starts, only birds and trees will hear your cries.

Don't rely on weak walls and fabric to protect you from the dark forces of the deep woods. Vacant cabins and remote campsites are ideal hiding spots for escaped convicts, restless spirits, and supernatural creatures.

Don't let that scare you away from the wilderness, though. I invite you to explore it for yourself: return to nature, challenge your instincts, test your fitness, and face the terrors and strangeness of the woods.

This section's tales serve as a reminder that the disquieting mysteries of the wilderness can intrude upon your cabin or tent, whether you're alone or not. And out there, *you* are your only salvation.

THE VISITORS

We all dream of a plot of land to call our own. Somewhere to put
a cozy cabin and camp with loved ones. Unbeknownst to us, the land we claim
is not rightfully ours, and its true owners may not be pleased with us.

FIELD NOTES

Location: A dense forest in Utah, USA
Date/Time: A night with a full moon overhead
Atmosphere: The air is full of potential, rife with wonder . . . then eroded by malice

This incident happened to me not long after I came across a listing for forty acres
(16 ha) of recreational land in a heavily forested area of Utah, approximately nine
thousand feet (2,743 m) above sea level. The land was a steal, priced at only $1,000 USD
per acre, but there were no utilities. It shared a border with approximately two million
acres (807,371 ha) of BLM (Bureau of Land Management) land, miles of forest that would
never be torn down or harvested. It was perfect.

A friend and I made a deal, and we went in fifty-fifty on the land. We split the
property but agreed we had no issues sharing our halves with each other since we were
buddies and wanted our families to always have fun experiences camping out there.
I parked a camper on the land, and we split the cost to build a rustic cabin. Basically, a
four hundred-square-foot (37 m²) cabin with a wood-burning stove, a porch, and some
bunk beds. As we settled into the cabin for the night, we eagerly chatted about our plans
to invite our families on our inaugural camping adventure.

We must have fallen asleep.

THE FOOTSTEPS GOT CLOSER, SLOWLY, UNTIL I COULD SEE THE LARGE FIGURE OF A MAN STANDING IN THE WINDOW FRAME. HIS SHOULDERS ROSE AND DROPPED WITH EACH BREATH.

I awoke to the sound of someone rummaging through the back of my truck. We were a mile or two (2 to 3 km) from the nearest parcel owned by anyone, so I was shocked someone was in our camp. I quietly woke up my buddy. The rummaging persisted, accompanied by the high-pitched squeak of the truck's suspension, and echoing footsteps drawing nearer to the cabin.

I could then hear a deep and guttural breathing. It sounded powerful. We had built the cabin a foot (30 cm) off the ground. We cut out a window approximately seven feet (2 m) high at the top of the window.

It was a full moon, and our campground was well-lit. The footsteps got closer, slowly, until I could see the large figure of a man standing in the window frame. His shoulders rose and dropped with each breath. You would have to be a minimum of six feet (2 m) tall to be visible in that window. This was a big dude.

To dispel our fear, my friend yelled, "Identify yourself. We're armed!"

The figure then turned and walked away, never to visit us again.

When we woke up the next morning, we discovered that it had rifled through my truck, tossing everything aside but leaving the valuables behind.

When examining the windows of my truck, the sight of immense handprints astonished us, as they dwarfed even my large friend's hands.

We've started to think that perhaps who we encountered wasn't human.

Utah is no stranger to the presence of Bigfoot. One family even caught on video what people believe to be this infamous cryptid.

This video has gained significant attention in the Bigfoot community, with experts analyzing the footage frame by frame. It shows Bigfoots that exhibit the characteristic traits: tall, hairy, and walking on two legs. Witnesses who have encountered Bigfoot in Utah describe them as shy and elusive creatures, often leaving behind large footprints and distinct odors. Strange vocalizations in the mountains support belief in Bigfoot in remote Utah. Despite the skepticism surrounding Bigfoot sightings, the prevalence of encounters in Utah, along with the compelling video evidence, continues to captivate and intrigue both believers and skeptics alike.

GLOWING EYES

Children always whisper tall tales to each other, from one ear to the next. Stories created to scare one another with tales of monsters and evils. However, the fact that adolescents are the ones conveying the story should not undermine its significance.

FIELD NOTES

Location: A rundown campground, anywhere
Date/Time: The annual family camping trip, in 2008
Atmosphere: Pine-scented air and the pleasantness of making new friends

This story has stuck with me for a long time. It takes place when I was on a family camping trip. I don't remember exactly where we were. It was some spot my mother had heard about from a friend. It was not a place we had been before, but the friend offered us their RV to go spend a few nights there and see if we liked it.

This camping spot was way out of the way. My mom's friend had to draw a map for us to find it. It was an actual campground, but I don't remember the name anymore. It was kind of rundown and gave me a weird vibe. Like that feeling you get when something is off, but you have no clue what it is.

Well, I was young, and I figured I just had that feeling because I'd never been here before. Now, we weren't the only people there. In the area we picked to put the RV, I could see maybe four or five other spots that were being used.

This RV was like your basic RV in 2008. A big bed in the back and a bunk over the driver's area. There was a couch too. That's where the sleeping spots were. At that age, I liked to climb. I was like a little monkey. So I took the bunk over the driving area. It had

a big window in the front of it for me to look out. I could close this little curtain, but it was partially see-through. If it were daylight, I could see people through it, but not very clearly, just their outlines.

The RV was situated by this spot right next to the river. We used to do a lot of fishing, so I thought that was great. I wouldn't have to carry all my fishing stuff very far.

I jumped at the chance to go fishing right away. We set everything up with the RV, and I was heading for the river. It was maybe twentyish feet (6 m) from our campsite. I set up my seat, then got my pole ready and baited the hook. In doing so, I pricked my finger a lot because the damn worm was so wiggly. Then again, all worms are.

I got my hook baited, cast it out, and sat down to wait. I waited until my butt got sore, doing the usual reeling in to make sure there was still bait. The fish were being crafty and kept getting away with my bait, so I had to keep re-baiting the hook. You know how fishing is. During all this, I noticed a few others fishing farther down. We weren't close, but not that far.

I decided to be friendly and called out, "Catching anything?"

A boy, about my age, was the one to call back. "I got a catfish about an hour ago, but nothing since!"

"Something keeps stealing my bait!" I responded, my voice echoing from the trees.

"What bait are you using?"

"Just some worms. You?"

"Chicken liver," he replied. We continued to talk (well, call back) to each other about fishing.

Just because I do a little fishing does not mean I can identify the fish. A bass, a catfish, a bluegill, those I can tell, but I cannot tell you if you're holding a trout or not.

This boy, whom we'll call Leo, was nice, and walked over to show me a little pamphlet of fish he had with him. We sat together for hours after that, talking and fishing. Leo and his family were only two spots away from mine, along the river. After giving up on fishing for the day, Leo asked if I wanted to hike with him.

By this time in my life, I had a cell phone. So, when I asked my parents if it was okay to go on a hike with my new friend, they said yes. I packed a bag with water bottles and lunch. I met up with Leo and we walked to the trailhead. He told me it was his first time being at this campground too, but his uncle—whom he was with—came here all the time. So, of course, I had to ask about what his uncle thought of the place.

"Oh, Uncle says he loves coming here because he gets good proof," Leo chimed.

Proof? That had me interested. "Proof of what?"

"Something he calls Bigfoot, but I don't think that's what it really is."

I frowned, my skepticism painted on my face. "Do you not believe in Bigfoot?"

"It's not like that," Leo assured me. "I just think he's using the wrong name for it."

That statement piqued my curiosity. I adjusted my bag and asked Leo, "What makes you think that? Have you seen it?"

"Well, no, I haven't seen it myself. But my uncle tells me about it," Leo explained. "He says it's really tall and hairy. That it has enormous feet and makes these weird sounds, and it has a foul smell when it's close."

So far, to me, that sounded like Bigfoot. But I wanted to know more before just saying that's what I thought it was. I asked him what else his uncle said about it.

That's when I was completely surprised. Leo told me his uncle said this thing had a tail and would howl on full moons. Of course, howling at a full moon made me think: werewolf. Though, I don't think we have those in Iowa. I could be wrong. The more Leo told me, the more it made me think. This sounded like a mix of things. Wolf and Bigfoot. Was that a possibility? Was he talking about a wolfman?

Keep in mind, I was still young, and into learning about cryptids and folkloric monsters. So, I was excited about this; so long as the sun was still in the sky, anyway. It's like when the sun is out, that stuff doesn't scare you.

But that safety was slowly stripped away when we stopped to eat our lunches and we saw just how deep into the trees we had walked. We couldn't even hear the river anymore. I told Leo we should head back after we eat.

He agreed. We sat and ate, talking about hobbies and things like, "How many times have you done this or that?" and just things kids talked about.

About halfway through eating, Leo asked me, "Did you hear that?"

I had heard nothing, so I shook my head. "No. What'd you hear?"

Leo listened closely but shook his head. "Never mind. Probably just a deer or something."

Now, my hyperactive imagination instantly thought, "Oh, hell no. That wasn't some deer!"

But I didn't say that. I just nodded. Besides, I hadn't heard the sound, so I couldn't say it wasn't a deer or some other normal animal. Let's just say we finished eating with haste and headed back. On the way, we didn't say anything. I think both of us were trying to see if we could hear anything. I'm not proud to admit it, but I started to pick up the pace when we heard something moving behind us.

"You hear that?" I nervously whispered.

"Yeah. Sounded big. Do you think someone else is out here hiking?"

"Oh, sure." My words felt empty. I could tell neither of us really believed that.

I think we were trying to keep each other from freaking out. When we got back, we just kind of chuckled at how silly we were. What were the odds the Bigfoot, as his uncle called it, was out there watching the two of us eating? That stuff happens in scary movies, not real life.

A mixture of Bigfoot and a werewolf, capable of large scratches in trees, and eyes glowing like an animal? Could our culprit for this encounter be the world-famous Dogman? Legend of the Dogman sparked back in 1987, when a man living in the village of Luther, Michigan, USA, filed a police report regarding a massive dog attacking his isolated cabin.

The isolated cabin attack sparked widespread curiosity and fear. The creature responsible for the cabin's destruction intrigued people; and as the story gained traction, more individuals shared their encounters with it. One particularly chilling account came from a man who claimed to have encountered the creature in the 1930s while fishing. These stories further fascinated and solidified the Dogman's status as an eerie legend that captured the nation's imagination.

Of course, when these things happen to you, your brain seeks rational explanations. Monsters watching their prey from beyond the trees only happens on TV. Well, I was telling myself that. I get spooked easily sometimes.

We headed to our campsites. I thought about telling my parents about what Leo told me about his uncle, but I knew they'd just laugh. So, I kept it to myself. After I got back, I spent the rest of the day fishing until I had to help make dinner. Overall, my first day wasn't that bad.

It was the nighttime I should've worried about.

That evening, we made and ate s'mores and I took a shower. After drying off, I climbed up in my bed and closed the curtain. Even though I was comfortable, falling asleep has always been difficult for me. I was lying on my side, just looking at the window. To avoid being yelled at by my parents, I had my music playing and listened with headphones. I was just kind of waiting for sleep to take me.

After I don't know how long, I got a weird feeling.

Don't ask me why, but I pulled off my headphones and peeked out the curtain. It wasn't a full moon, but it was pretty darn close to it. So, there was a fair amount of light. I saw what I thought were fireflies.

Then I noticed they were too big and staying too still.

They were in a position that was slightly too elevated—but having witnessed them reach such heights before, it wasn't too concerning.

I watched them for a moment. They just sat there for I don't know how long. My elbow got sore from leaning on it for a while. I tried to ignore them. I told myself I was all worked up because of what Leo said. It happened all the time when I heard creepy stories and stuff. So, I told myself that's what was happening, and I rolled over. I fell asleep at some point.

I told Leo the next morning, "I think you got me freaked out yesterday by telling me about your uncle's Bigfoot."

Leo was a little confused. "Why? Did you have a dream about it?"

I shook my head. "No, but I swear I saw eyes in the trees last night. Pretty silly, huh?"

"What color were they?" Leo said, glaring at me.

That caught me off guard. "What?"

IF YOU SEE THE EYES, YOU SHOULDN'T GO OUT AT NIGHT.

"What color were they?"

I just shrugged. "I don't know. Like when you shine the light in an animal's eyes at night, I guess. Dude, you had me worked up. It was probably just my brain playing tricks or a raccoon."

I think I was trying to make myself feel better at this point. Leo just said, "Don't go out at night and stay close to your campsite."

Well, that both confused me and scared me. "What? Why?"

"My uncle says so. If you see the eyes, you shouldn't go out at night."

It freaked me out. I didn't know what to do. I just told Leo, "You shouldn't scare me because it will freak me out for weeks."

He just said, "Then let's talk about something else."

I was more than happy to change the subject. We started talking about things like our pets, and we went fishing. Well, he fished, and I sat with him and talked. I spent most of the day with Leo when I was there.

But at night, I was a wreck. I would look out from the curtain at night and see the eyes in the trees. Finally, I got a hold of Leo and told him to come with me to check where I had seen the eyes at night. We walked into the weeds and trees.

At first, we saw nothing. But then we saw where the grass and weeds were all stomped down, like someone had been standing there. There were deep scratch marks on a tree. Like maybe when you put your hand against something to lean on it. I mean, why would something just claw a tree like that for no reason?

I looked at Leo. "What's this?"

I pointed at the scratches. Leo shook his head. I got uneasy and decided to get back to my campsite. We spent the day in camp. We didn't even go to the river. I don't know why, I just felt like I should be close to the RV in case I had to run. I'm not a fast runner. That last day there was just spent shifting around and glancing at the trees while trying to talk about anything but the Bigfoot creature.

My family left the next day, but that last night will stick with me. I checked for the eyes again, which I had done every night for the last few nights. That final time, I didn't see any eyes. I'd seen them every night until this night. I thought I was fine. While closing the curtain, I noticed something in my peripheral vision.

Keep in mind, I was already jumpy. I looked and saw something big near the river. It was covered in what looked like fur.

I saw what looked like a tail. I became terrified. So, as any smart kid would do, I closed the curtain and pulled the blanket over my head. I had not a single moment of sleep that night. I heard something outside a few times, but I stayed under the blanket. I was too scared to look. What would happen if it spotted me? What would it do? What was it?

When I got out of bed the next morning, I didn't even get dressed. I walked out in my pajamas, not caring that it was just a big shirt that draped over my shorts. I looked around and saw prints. It looked like a mix of people's feet and a paw. I knew then that it wasn't my imagination that night.

After my family packed up camp, I bid Leo farewell. We never went back there. We preferred our usual campground, anyway. But I still wonder, what could that have been? What did it want? Was there more than one out there? Was there only one, or did it have like a family unit? I wasn't aware of any physical damage it caused.

But that doesn't mean there wasn't any.

The song titled "The Legend" was written and performed by disc jockey Steve Cook, who claimed to have received numerous calls from radio listeners sharing their encounters with the Michigan Dogman. The song quickly became a local sensation, sparking curiosity and excitement among the community.

People describe the creature in various ways, but they often depict it as a bipedal, wolflike creature standing anywhere from six to eight feet (2 m) tall. Some witnesses claim it has glowing red eyes and emits a chilling howl that echoes through the woods. Despite the skepticism surrounding the existence of the Michigan Dogman, sightings and reports of encounters continue to surface.

MY GREAT-GRANDMOTHER'S HORROR STORY

An elderly woman recounts to her grandson a story
from the Wild West. A time of cowboys, bandits, and a specter stuck
between worlds, traveling the Plains for its next victim.

FIELD NOTES

Location: The Wild West, USA
Date/Time: Long ago, in the nineteenth century
Atmosphere: Gritty, lawless, and malevolent

When a lot of us think of the 1800s, we tend to think of cheesy rhinestone cowboy TV shows. We don't think about how terrifying it truly was to be alive at that time. And a story my great-grandmother told me has forced me to rethink my fanciful visions of the past.

I was born in 1959 and did not meet my great-grandmother until I was around seven, so it would have been 1966, I believe. My great-grandmother, who at the time was around ninety-eight, was a very sweet and kind little old lady.

She dressed how I had seen people dress on the TV show *Bonanza*. So, for a young child who was obsessed with stories of the "Wild West" that I had seen on TV, I was so excited to flood her with questions.

At first, she told me these wondrous stories of covered wagons, cowboy shootouts, building everything you owned, and just general stories of living in a mostly lawless time. It was the middle of summer, and my mother had told me to take my dog out to the backyard so he could use the facilities, and then we could get settled in for the night.

Within a few seconds of my mother saying this, my great-grandmother jumped to her feet from her chair and screamed, "No! Don't let him go out there!"

My grandmother walked over, put a hand on her shoulder, and whispered something in her ear to settle her down. It was kind of alarming to me because I didn't really know this woman too well.

But being a silly kid, I wrote it off and took Rowdy out to the backyard. When I got back in and locked up, the mood had completely changed. Even though I was going to be allowed to stay up later than normal, my mom told me to take Rowdy and go to bed.

I questioned my mom and asked what was going on, as I could see that my great-grandmother was very disturbed in the other room. My mother said, "Jacob, go to bed!"

I was not familiar with her carrying that tone toward me, so I obeyed. I lay down after putting my pajamas on and just looked at the ceiling, not really able to sleep.

I went downstairs to get some milk and maybe sneak some of the sweets my family had made earlier that day. But then I saw my great-grandmother sitting by the window, lost in thought. I asked her, "Grandma Caroline, is everything okay?"

She turned around and looked at me and said, "Do you want to know why I didn't want you to go outside?"

I said, "Yes, please!" Believing I was about to hear another "Wild West" story, I grabbed my sweets cautiously, not knowing what she would say, and sat down for a story.

She continued, voice rasped by the passage of time, "The reason I didn't want you to go outside is because I didn't want him to get you. I've seen it twice since I've been here, and I won't let it happen again."

"What are you talking about, Grandma Caroline?" I said, trying to wrap my childlike wonder around her vague mumblings.

"The black Haint in the woods." She replied.

"What is a Haint?"

"It can mean a lot of things, but at its core, it means something evil," she said, "When I was seventeen, in 1885, I saw it for the first time."

What follows is the story from her childhood, as she told it to me.

"My daddy, who was a Civil War veteran, took me, my sisters, and my mama on a bit of a trip to meet some men he had served with in the war. Along the way, we had to set up camp a couple of times, but we didn't mind because we were too caught up in the excitement of the whole thing! It was in the middle of summer, so we let Mama and Daddy have the tent, and me and my sisters slept on blankets and looked up at the stars and just dreamed.

"On the second night, when we were settling in for camp, a family of travelers on their way through the area stopped by and asked if they could share the area for their camp. My daddy was a superb judge of character, and he didn't sense anything strange, so he agreed—so long as everyone minded their own business. They made their camp quickly and fell asleep almost as fast. I had woken up late in the night to see the youngest boy of the group walking toward the woods.

"At first, I couldn't tell what he was walking toward, but I knew he didn't need to be up and about. I quickly lit a small lantern to run after him and see what was going on, almost afraid I was going to catch him pissing out by the tree line when I saw it.

"A tall, dark man with a long trench coat and big hat.

"Like the men that we would see coming through town from time to time, looking to pick a fight or start some trouble.

"At first, I thought it was a real man and told him to mind his own business. When he looked up though, I knew it was something evil! His eyes were bright white and when he smiled, from his mouth protruded a bright, ethereal steam that shouldn't have been possible in the middle of summer.

"Before I could even react, he had grabbed the boy and was gone! Suddenly, I fainted and came to the next morning, during a search to find the boy. He was gone, and nobody ever found him. I told my daddy about everything that had happened. He told me to forget about it and that we were going home right away.

"I couldn't make sense of anything that happened. After we got home late the next night, my daddy directed us all straight to bed! I tried to lie there and sleep but couldn't get it off my mind.

"Then I heard something rustling in the woods. I looked out my window and I saw it again! That son of a bitch with those white eyes, looking directly at me! I rubbed my eyes several times to make sure I was awake, and he was still there! I ran to my mama and daddy's room to get my daddy—and he was gone!

"But then I noticed the front door was open. I walked to the open door and saw my daddy sitting on the porch with a mouthful of tobacco and a shotgun in his hand, facing the side of the house. He didn't even turn his head to speak to me.

"He said he knew what I'd been seeing. That he had started seeing it after coming home from the war. That it'd been around for years and I shouldn't worry about it.

"I told him I couldn't do that and sat there next to him. This godless thing stared at us all night before eventually turning and walking back into the woods before the sun broke. We would sit and watch it, just me and Daddy, almost every night for months when suddenly, he just stopped appearing.

"Not long after, I met your great-granddaddy, got married, and moved away. I didn't see the man again until the night that your great-great-granddaddy died. He was lying on his deathbed at his and Mama's house; I looked out the window— and just as sure as I was standing there, so was that terrifying creature.

Haints are believed to be restless spirits that have not found peace and are trapped between the worlds of the living and the dead. They are often described as pale or blue, and some legends say they can take the form of a mist or a light. Haints are said to haunt specific locations, such as old houses, graveyards, or bodies of water.

Legends say Haints can be particularly active during the night and people can deter them by taking certain protective measures, such as painting porch ceilings or door frames blue or hanging up bottle trees. The Gullah Geechee people, who are primarily of West and Central African heritage, have passed down stories and beliefs about Haints for generations, intertwining their own experiences and traditions with elements of European folklore.

HIS EYES WERE BRIGHT WHITE AND WHEN HE SMILED, FROM HIS MOUTH PROTRUDED A BRIGHT, ETHEREAL STEAM THAT SHOULDN'T HAVE BEEN POSSIBLE IN THE MIDDLE OF SUMMER.

"After Daddy died, I didn't see the man again until the night that we pulled up in your driveway when I saw him standing in the bushes beside your house. I don't know what he is, Jacob, and I don't know what he wants. So just make sure you stay in the house after dark and keep that damn dog in the house, too."

As her story petered out, I could feel my nerves on edge. At this point, I was far too afraid to go back to sleep. So I just held Rowdy as tight as I could and lay there. The next morning, on little to no sleep, I walked down the stairs to find Grandma Caroline and everybody else laughing and joking as if nothing had ever happened.

When I questioned her about the conversation that she and I had the night before, she said, "I'm sorry, honey, I don't know what you're talking about."

But then, a few moments later, she looked at me with a very distinct look and gave me a wink. The rest of Grandma Caroline's visit was uneventful.

She left two days later, and although she would live to be 102 years old, that was the first and only time I would ever see her. To this day, I look into the dark to try to see if I can catch a glimpse of whatever this thing is—and I never have. Maybe that's for the best.

Although Grandma Caroline died peacefully in her home, my Aunt Whitney said her last words were, "I see him standing there . . ."

HIS GUARDIAN ANGEL

It's easy to long for the voice of a lost loved one. To hear just one more word, to hear them laugh again. And should the ethereal voice make itself known? The words whispered through the veil would demand the utmost respect.

FIELD NOTES

Location: Far enough in the woods for someone to get lost, anywhere
Date/Time: A recent camping trip
Atmosphere: Solemn, heavy with longing

Ghosts aren't always malevolent. Some are downright gentle, just like the one in this experience of mine. This was one of the last times I went camping, and I was with my cousin, his girlfriend, and my boyfriend. My cousin Russell, thirty-nine at the time of this story, was my favorite family member since he always went out of his way for me. To make this story make sense, I need to tell you about my former roommate as well.

Her name was Alice, and she and Russell were always so sweet together. When he was thirty-three, my roommate and I were both twenty-two. Alice and Russell often played pranks on each other, like how he would pour cold water on Alice while she showered, or she would hide around the house to startle him.

But whenever we were all watching a movie, Alice would always sit next to him and rest her head on his shoulder. Now, my cousin is peculiar with people putting their head on his shoulder, so only the people he truly loves may do so. One day, we heard Alice had been in a terrible accident and was in the hospital.

When we arrived at the hospital, Alice's family was sitting in the hallway. The doctor asked if we were Gabby and Russell, which we confirmed. The doctor said, "She won't make it long, so please make it short." When we saw Alice, my heart stopped.

They had wired her to so many machines. However, Alice smiled and stuck out her hand to grab Russell's. He sat next to the bed on a stool and I walked to the edge of the bed. She told me, "I love you, Gabs," and then turned her head to Russell. She grabbed the bracelet she was wearing and, placing it in Russell's hand, said, "I love you so much. I wish we could have been together, but I'll always be with you."

After she said that, her heart monitor flatlined, and sadly, she died right in front of our eyes. My cousin wears that bracelet every day and only takes it off when showering, bathing, or swimming. He also got a tattoo with her name and angel wings on his right pec.

Three years later, and my cousin Russell finally got a girlfriend. Eloise and Russell had been an official couple for three months, and my boyfriend Eddy and I had been together for a full year.

Eddy wanted to go camping with me, and I suggested Russell and Eloise come with us. Since Eddy and Russell were like two peas in a pod when they were together, Russell agreed. The next day, Eloise and Russell showed up with camping equipment, and we went to the biggest forest nearby. After setting up camp and cooking the food we brought, we sat on the ground telling each other ghost stories. Then we turned in for the night.

Little did I know I would soon be telling my own ghost story.

The next day, I was the first one to wake up. As I got out of the tent, Eloise was also coming out of the tent she and Russell shared. She turned to us and said, "Good morning. Have you seen my boyfriend?"

"No, I thought I was the first one awake," I replied to her and looked around, trying to spot Russell, but I couldn't.

A few hours passed, and there was still no sign of Russell. I could see Eloise was getting restless.

Surely there are kind spirits out there. But can they really reach through the veil to help those in need? Well, turns out it isn't too uncommon a practice. Despite much controversy, there are spirit mediums who attempt to help locate those who are lost by trying to channel spirits for information. Sure, most of the time it might be a scam preying on the vulnerable, but every time? Jessica Larson would beg to differ.

In April 2022, when Larson's son, Austin, went missing in the local woods of Skandia, Michigan, she contacted her friend Sarah Johnson, known for her psychic abilities. Johnson agreed to help and immediately began focusing her energy on locating Austin. Johnson used her intuition to guide search and rescue crews to specific areas in the woods. Despite the skepticism from some members of the search team, they followed Johnson's directions and were astonished to find Austin alive and well, huddled near a fallen tree. Jessica Larson expressed her gratitude for Johnson's help, stating that without her psychic abilities, they may have never found her son in time.

"Where could he be?" she said, worried.

I put my hand on her leg to comfort her and said, "He might have just fallen asleep somewhere." She managed a smile, but anyone could see that it was a fake smile out of worry.

Hours passed and Eloise finally called the cops. They organized a search party and graciously allowed the three of us to lend a hand. A few hours into the search, I saw something blinking in the remaining sunlight.

I walked up to it and saw that it was Alice's bracelet. My heart pounded, though I don't know if the beat was full of hope or despair. If the bracelet was there, then maybe he was nearby—but if it wasn't on him, maybe something ripped it off.

Still deep in my thoughts, I heard an officer shout my name. I reflexively put the bracelet into my pocket. I thought if they saw it, they might try to take it and I had a feeling, a familial sense, that I needed to hold on to it.

The officer informed us it would soon be dark, and they planned to search for him tomorrow with the dogs. I felt a sinking feeling in my heart because of my fear for my cousin's safety.

When I returned to the tent, I saw Eddy trying to calm Eloise, who was now crying. She didn't stop crying until she fell asleep. Now, with Eddy and me lying in bed, Eddy said, "We'll find him, okay? I'm sure he's alive and well, wherever he is." He kissed me and stroked my hair.

I lay on my back, trying to fall asleep, but it was clear I couldn't. Eddy was fast asleep, and I could hear Eloise's soft snoring coming from the tent next to ours. I picked up the bracelet and held it up, lamenting where my cousin was.

No sooner did I do that when a voice, as if carried by the wind, said, "Follow me."

I got up and said louder, "Hello, who's there?"

But I heard nothing. However, I felt the bracelet hit the side of my hand—which was weird since I hadn't moved. There was no wind in the tent.

If there are good and bad people, then there must be good and bad spirits. The good ones are the remnants of once-loving energy.

In Jewish folklore, the benevolent spirits known as Ibbur are believed to be righteous and compassionate beings. They are said to be the souls of deceased individuals who have not yet completed their spiritual journey or fulfilled their purpose in life. These spirits choose to enter the body of a living person temporarily to offer guidance, wisdom, and assistance. Ibbur are believed to possess individuals who are deemed worthy and in need of their help, often those facing challenges or seeking personal growth. These spirits bring positive energy, inspiration, and support to their hosts, helping them overcome obstacles and achieve their goals. The Ibbur's presence is a blessing and a sign of divine intervention, providing comfort and enlightenment to those fortunate enough to experience their influence.

"Follow me," I heard again. I put on my pants and grabbed my blouse.

I opened the tent and stood up, stepping out while buttoning my blouse. That's when I saw a figure standing in the distance. I couldn't see any features, but as I took a step forward, the figure took a step back, making no sound. I took another step forward, and the figure repeated its action, silently retreating.

Gathering my courage, I said, "Who are you?" But I didn't hear a response.

The bracelet hit the back of my leg, surprising me. I picked up the bracelet from the ground, and as I held it, I heard that windy voice say, "You can trust me."

I was mind-blown. Alice always said that to me when I was afraid of something. With my mouth wide open, I slowly got up while holding the bracelet.

Then I swallowed and gathered my courage yet again. I said, "Alice, is that you?" Then I heard a giggle. I smiled because I recognized that giggle. There was no mistaking it. It was Alice, and she was here to help. I started walking toward the figure, which I was now sure was my darling departed friend, Alice.

As I followed her, I tried asking her questions like, "Alice, where are you taking me?" But all I got in response were giggles. Then she stood still, and so did I.

"Come." I walked closer to the figure, and as I approached, it became clearer that it was indeed Alice. A tear stroked my cheek as I saw her standing in front of me, but she turned her face to the left.

"Go there," she said, so I walked toward where she was looking.

After a few steps, I noticed a hole in the ground and shouted, "Hello!" into the hole.

My cousin's voice shouted, "Gabs, is that you?"

His voice was distorted and quiet for a yell, like the dirt and forest were dampening the noise. It must have muffled the sound of our shouts as they traveled down to where he was.

I was so relieved and shouted, "Oh, my God, are you okay? What happened?"

"I fell and hurt my ankle badly. I can't even stand on it, but you need to help me out of this hole!" he shouted back.

I put the bracelet into my pocket, extended my hand into the hole, and Russell grabbed it. With my help, he managed to climb out of the hole.

I PICKED UP THE BRACELET FROM THE GROUND, AND AS I HELD IT, I HEARD THAT WINDY VOICE SAY, "YOU CAN TRUST ME."

He looked at me and asked, "How did you find me, Gabs?"

I grabbed the bracelet out of my pocket, showed it to him, and said, "Guess who."

He smiled and said, "It was Alice, huh?"

I smiled and said, "Yes, I saw her, and she led me to you."

Then I heard her say, "Love you."

I turned to Russell and asked him, "Did you hear that?"

He smiled and said, "Yes, I did." He looked straight ahead, as if seeing something beyond our sight.

As I supported him, we walked back to the tents. Halfway there, the sun rose. I asked him, "How did you end up in that hole?"

"Well, as I was picking up wood to start the breakfast fire, I ran into a boar and stupidly started running," he replied.

I looked at him directly, and he smiled sheepishly as he confessed, "The boar chased after me, and I tried dodging through the trees, but it kept pursuing me. I hit a few trees; that's probably how I lost the bracelet. But I kept running."

The forest was bathed in a golden glow as a ray of sunlight broke through the canopy. Russell and I sighed and looked at each other, smiling. Russell and I embraced, and he told me, "Alice longed to witness the sunlight streaming through the trees like this."

We both heard the voice again, saying, "Thank you."

We turned around and saw Alice standing there, looking at us. Then we heard Eloise shouting as she ran toward us.

She threw her arms around Russell, crying her eyes out and kissing him like crazy. Eddy hugged me, said, "My God, where were you, and where did you find him?"

We told them how I found him, omitting the parts where Alice helped.

Russell still wears the bracelet every day and even named his first daughter Alice. She's now a year and seven months old. When she is old enough, he plans to have his daughter wear the bracelet and have Alice be her guardian angel.

MIDDLE OF NOWHERE

You ever drive through a stretch of road and stumble upon a single home miles away from anyone else? I wonder what it would be like to live in such a place—comfy, quiet, perhaps a little lonely. But scarce grocery store trips and unanswered emergency service requests are some of the scary aspects of living in the middle of nowhere.

"Nowhere" in this case refers to being surrounded by wilderness for miles (or kilometers, as the case may be). You name it: deserts, forests, swampland, or prairies. In the middle of nowhere, you are your last line of defense.

It makes me curious about the thoughts of predatory individuals when they come across such a remote dwelling. Do they see the residents as easy prey? Are they tempted to peek inside?

Stay alert when walking outside at night in isolated areas. There may be unexpected hazards. The stories contained in this section illustrate a terrifying picture of who or what seeks to turn your faraway home into a nightmare hellscape.

THE OLD GAS STATION

The building looks like it hasn't seen human life in decades. Only the small skittering of insects and rodents have kept the place company. So why is it you could swear you just heard someone stepping behind you?

NOTES

Location: The wilds of Colorado, USA
Date/Time: An evening in late spring
Atmosphere: A pensive isolation, the presence of a stranger

I'm what many people may call a drifter. You're free to use whatever term you like. I have been wandering the country since I graduated high school, jumping from place to place, finding work wherever I can get it. It's not what a person would call "stable living," but I do what I can to get by.

Living on a budget of a drifter isn't always comfortable, especially since hotels are so expensive these days; most nights, I must find somewhere to camp. I enjoy the experience, especially on late spring nights when it's cool out and you can gaze off into the stars as you fall asleep.

It was on such a night that this series of occurrences happened. I was in a small town in Colorado. It was about 7:30 p.m. when I noticed the sun going down. As per routine, I walked into the woods looking for a place to camp. I was extra careful in choosing a camping spot this evening and ended up walking a long way into the Colorado wilderness. It was a pleasant walk with lots of nature to see, until I found something strange.

"A gas station?" I whispered to myself.

BUT BEFORE I COULD THINK OF ANYTHING, THE GROWLING STOPPED, AND A DEEP, DISTORTED VOICE REPEATED TO ME, "WHAT COULD IT BE?" AS IF IT WAS TRYING TO IMITATE ME.

After walking for so long, surrounded by unfamiliar trees and plants, it surprised me to stumble upon an old, rusty gas station in the middle of nowhere. The place was in shambles and looked like it would fall over at the mere sign of wind. The gas station's design suggested that it was constructed in the '60s. Nevertheless, the place was rickety, so it was too much of a risk that the building would collapse on me if I slept inside.

However, Mother Nature wasn't having it, and soon the pitter-patter of raindrops filled the air. Left with the circumstances, and with night rapidly approaching, I took shelter inside the gas station. As I passed through the front door, the sound of rain smacking the metal roof echoed in my ears. I immediately saw a large countertop with shelves behind it. To my left, there was a door that went into the garage portion of the station.

The whole place was empty, filled only with a strange smell and cracked black-and-white tiles for flooring. It wasn't the coziest of places, but it beat sleeping in the rain. Apart from it being a dump, the garage door had a bent part that left a small opening, inviting unwelcome guests like snakes to sneak in—and the last thing I wanted was to be bitten in my sleep. So, I decided to sleep to the right of the counter, in front of the main door, using my sleeping bag as a mattress.

As soon as I lay down, an unsettling feeling washed over me, urging me to leave immediately—as if there was an imminent threat or danger lurking nearby. I ignored this feeling and allowed the exhaustion of walking all day to lull me to sleep.

. . . What a mistake that was.

I awoke to the sound of growling outside of the building. It took me a while, but as soon as I realized what I was hearing, I became fully alert. Due to previous

Urbex, or urban exploration, originated in the 1970s when daring, curious individuals, driven to uncover secrets and untold stories, began exploring abandoned buildings and forgotten spaces. They explored decrepit structures, rooftops, and underground tunnels, documenting their experiences through photography. Over time, this unique subculture grew in popularity, attracting a diverse community of enthusiasts who share a passion for unveiling the hidden treasures of urban landscapes. Today, urbex has developed into a worldwide phenomenon, with urban explorers continuously seeking new locations and pushing the boundaries of exploration.

encounters with wolves and bears, I developed a habit of carrying a knife for self-defense. With the knife in hand, I strained my ears to decipher the source of the menacing growls. It didn't sound like a bear; it sounded bigger. The growls were some of the deepest I'd ever heard a creature make.

"What could it be?" I said to myself.

But before I could think of anything, the growling stopped, and a deep, distorted voice repeated to me, "What could it be?" as if it was trying to imitate me.

Quickly, I rushed to roll up my sleeping bag and placed it inside my backpack. While I continued packing up my other things, the sharp sound of the metal garage door being forcefully bent and lifted made me cringe. I put on my backpack and ran out the front door through the rain and into the woods. While I was running, I swear I could hear that same deep, distorted voice laughing loudly in the distance. I'm not sure how long I ran, but eventually, I made it back to the small town where I went looking for the police.

The local sheriff was parked next to a diner in his patrol vehicle. I guess he could tell I was a bit shaken, so he brought me into the diner, sat me down in a booth, and bought me a meal. Once I had finished my meal and had calmed my nerves, I told the sheriff what had happened.

He laughed, looked out of the window, took a sip of his coffee, and spoke.

"The old gas station, huh? Yeah, that place is *not* abandoned."

THE CLIMBING CRYPTID

Fingers are wrapped around the cold metal rung of the ladder. A man fights to secure his only chance of escape. There's only one way off the boat and it's the ladder . . . if he can fight off whatever is on the other end, wresting control of it.

FIELD NOTES

Location: Seabrook, New Hampshire, USA
Date/Time: Between 2015 and 2016, after a Saturday-night party
Atmosphere: Uncomfortable, isolated, dank, and dark

This incident happened to me around 2015 or 2016. I had just gotten out of a long-term relationship with a girl I met online. During that relationship, I lived with her in Connecticut, bordering Webster, Massachusetts.

After the breakup, I returned to Seabrook, New Hampshire, where I had grown up. I had no money and few belongings to speak of, but I knew lots of contractors and friends of the family who owned paving companies, so there was no shortage of work.

I had no place to stay, so my friend let me stay in his thirty-foot (9 m) luxury boat on his property. It was tucked back into the surrounding woods, probably about twenty feet (6 m) from the grassy yard where it was propped up on stilts.

I had to use a twelve-foot (4 m) extension ladder to climb up onto the stern of the boat and then get inside. Every night, I would perform this ritual, pulling up the ladder to ensure no unwelcome visitors could ascend in the darkness. This precaution was necessary, as my mind was often filled with terrifying tales that lulled me to sleep.

One Saturday night, I was returning home to the boat after leaving one of my friend's parties. I had had a bit to drink, so I had a pleasant buzz going. I'm not into any drugs

and I do not smoke weed because it gives me awful anxiety, even from one hit. So even though I wasn't 100 percent sober, I was still aware of what was happening— and I swear that what happened next actually did.

As I approached the boat, I got an eerie feeling, the one that we all try to brush off as nonsense. Nonetheless, I quickened my pace and got up the ladder as quickly as possible. It was the same feeling I'd get as a kid, turning the lights off and running up the stairs to escape monsters.

As I climbed over the top of the ladder into the back of the boat, I began to hear footsteps racing toward the boat. In response, I hastily grabbed the ladder and began to haul it up. When I got the ladder halfway up, I pushed down on my end to teeter the other end up in the air, getting it as high as I could as quickly as possible.

As I did this, something grabbed the lower end of the ladder and jerked it down, flinging my end of the ladder upwards and smashing my funny bone, causing me to roar out in pain. In the same instance, I smashed all my weight down on my end of the ladder, dropping all my dead weight onto it.

Thankfully, I must have weighed more than whatever the thing was because the ladder teetered in my favor. I peered at the other end of the ladder, and in the dim moonlight, I could see long, skinny wrists and two little hands gripping the last rung.

The fingers were rather short and stubby, with dirty nails, and the skin seemed to be gray.

SOMETHING GRABBED THE LOWER END OF THE LADDER AND JERKED IT DOWN, FLINGING MY END OF THE LADDER UPWARDS AND SMASHING MY FUNNY BONE, CAUSING ME TO ROAR OUT IN PAIN.

While we don't know for certain what this individual encountered, it could have been the Devil Monkey of Danville, New Hampshire. While people say Devil Monkeys have fur, they also resemble primates, so perhaps a juvenile Devil Monkey wouldn't have developed fur yet, exposing only the gray skin underneath.

Devil Monkeys have been sighted in the USA since the 1930s. Witnesses often describe encountering these creatures in remote wooded areas or near abandoned buildings. The Devil Monkey is known for its aggressive behavior and piercing red eyes, making it a formidable creature. Some reports even claim that the Devil Monkey emits a chilling screech or a bloodcurdling howl, further adding to its eerie persona. Cryptozoologists extensively study these sightings, collecting evidence like footprints and hair samples to support the existence of this elusive, primate-like creature. Despite their efforts, the origins and true nature of the Devil Monkey remain shrouded in mystery.

To be honest, they looked like they belonged to Gollum from the Lord of the Rings movies. When the ladder was level with the boat, the creature let go, causing me and the ladder to smash down in the back of the boat. I immediately scrambled to my feet and pulled the ladder farther up onto the boat so that nothing could jump up and grab it.

I didn't have a flashlight, but I saw a figure with gray eyes looking up at me. I quickly moved away so it couldn't see me. But it began running back and forth, to and from the boat. It would get maybe thirty or forty feet (9 or 12 m) away, turn around, and run straight back at me. It began making a loud gurgling, screaming noise that warbled like a turkey's call. That's probably the best way that I can describe it.

I stopped watching it running back and forth while making the noise; I was too freaked out. So, I sat and listened from the doorway, entering the lower half of the inside of the boat, getting ready to slam and lock the door at a moment's notice. This went on for about fifteen minutes until it finally ran off farther into the woods, and I never saw or heard from it again.

THE CLIMBING CRYPTID

THE PINYON SKINWALKER

Letting cool air drift into the room, she works away until interrupted by a noise. Outside her window, the animals she's used to are gone, and in their place is a beast of legend.

FIELD NOTES

Location: Off a dirt road, in the California desert, USA
Date/Time: A school night in the spring of 2022
Atmosphere: All alone, with the creeping sense that something in your surroundings is horrifically off

About a year ago, I used to live in a somewhat isolated little neighborhood that was in the high desert of California. I lived on a dirt road, and since the homes were so spread out, wildlife wasn't an uncommon thing. You'd see rabbits, coyotes, snakes, and—on rare occasions—deer.

Once you lived there for a while, you got used to animals roaming around during the late hours of the day. I'm Native American, so most of the time, I actually enjoyed seeing the wildlife so close to my home. But I always knew of a creature my tribe refers to as a "Skinwalker." I'm not supposed to say that word, but I typed it, so hopefully there's no bad omen. And that's what I think I saw in this story.

The house I lived in had a large backyard and a gravel mixed with dirt driveway, leaving a lot of open space to look out from. My room was at the front of the house, and every night, if I had my window open, I would find myself staring out at the front gate of our driveway. It was silent every night unless you heard coyote howls. There were a lot of strange things up there, and I wasn't the only one who experienced it. My boyfriend and my mother did as well.

IT WAS SO UNNATURAL, AND IT DIDN'T LOOK LIKE SOMETHING FROM THIS WORLD. THE SIGHT RESEMBLED A HUMAN IMITATING A DOG'S MOVEMENTS BY WALKING ON ALL FOURS.

While I was homeschooled, I sat in the office in silence, doing my work. In the silence, I swear I heard a knocking sound by the window that I could not see out of. I couldn't see through because we didn't have blinds or curtains. We had sliding barn doors as windows instead. I turned my head to look at the window and it went silent. Then I heard someone or something walking. Directly outside the window was gravel; I could hear the shifting of loose rocks.

It was footsteps. Not the sound of a rabbit or a coyote. It was definitely the footsteps of something larger. I froze because I didn't know what to do. Whatever was outside the window might hear me. After about five minutes, I left the computer and stayed in my room for the rest of the day. A month or two later, I changed rooms with the office to make it my bedroom. My bedroom originally was too small, and my father thought I needed more space.

One night, I was looking out the same window where I heard the footsteps. I was staring out at the gate that was blocking the opening to the driveway. I sometimes enjoyed looking out at the night sky, but this time, something had other plans.

After sitting there for about ten minutes stargazing, I saw a figure on the other side of the gate. It looked like a coyote, but it was too long, and the way it moved . . .

It was so unnatural, and it didn't look like something from this world. The sight resembled a human imitating a dog's movements by walking on all fours.

I wasn't scared at first, so I just waited to see what it was going to do. It was originally just walking past the gate like a normal coyote, but then it turned its head to look at the house. It was looking at me. I could just tell.

The eerie silhouette of a coyote-shaped creature emerged from the darkness, its eyes nowhere to be seen.

Talking about it makes me feel uneasy but here goes. It just stood there as still as a statue until it stood up on two legs and tried to climb over my goddamn gate. I lost it and rushed to shut the barn door windows, but that just seemed to make it angry. It started climbing faster. It made it onto my side of the gate. I heard it running toward my window before I closed it.

Once I did, it just—stopped. I had many other experiences in that house, but that was the last time I kept my window open at night. I haven't seen that creature since, and I'm happy I haven't. When my family moved out of that house, I was very sad, and I still miss it. I considered it my real home, but I am thankful I won't have to see that thing ever again.

Skinwalker belief is deeply rooted in western Indigenous culture and spirituality, especially within the Navajo tribe. In Navajo mythology, Skinwalkers could transform into any animal. However, the power to become a Skinwalker was not easily attained. It was believed that individuals could only gain this power through initiation into the Witchery Way, a secretive and often taboo practice within the tribe.

The initiation into the Witchery Way involved committing heinous acts, like murdering a close relative, especially a sibling. These acts symbolized severing familial ties and embracing darkness. Other crimes associated with the initiation included necrophilia and grave-robbing, further delving into the realm of the macabre and forbidden. Once an individual was initiated into the Witchery Way, they were considered to have become "pure evil," wielding supernatural abilities for malevolent purposes.

THE BLACK-EYED GIRL

Timid knocking against the front door echoes through the house. A woman, home alone, answers the door to find a lost child asking to be let in. Though something is off, an unsettling feeling cautions her against letting this child into her home.

FIELD NOTES

Location: The last house on the street, down a dirt road
Date/Time: 12:40 a.m. on a cool day in April, in the transition between the seasons
Atmosphere: Tense, panicked, distressed

I had a strange encounter with the BEC, or Black-Eyed Children. It was super creepy, to say the least. I lost some sleep over it. I may get scared easily, but this was the first time I felt a fear that you get when you think your life is in danger.

There aren't many houses near my home, which is located on a dirt road. I only have a few neighbors, and only one of them has kids. It's a peaceful place for the most part, and I used to like that. But ever since this incident happened, paranoia is constantly scratching at me.

It was warm for a night in the first week of April. But in the South, that isn't too uncommon. It was around 12:40 a.m., and I was awake, checking out my YouTube page and watching random stuff. Out of nowhere, I heard my big dog Bella growling at the front door. As someone with two dogs, three indoor cats, and one outdoor cat, I firmly believe that animals are more sensitive to the paranormal than humans are.

Bella's growling was unusual. She's a very friendly lab mix and never growls. So, I looked up from my computer and could have sworn I saw something through the glass border around my front door.

I tried to tell Bella to hush since the walls were paper thin, and that if she started barking, she'd wake the rest of my family. Bella calmed down when she heard my

voice, but stayed put at the front door. I thought everything was okay after that. But ten minutes later, Bella's growls filled the room once more, causing my cats to fixate on the front door, their unblinking eyes locked in anticipation. It was like they saw something there that I didn't see.

So, this time I got up from my bed (my bed is in the living room for past medical reasons), and as I took a couple of steps toward the door, I heard a light knocking. Bella started growling a little louder at this, and I immediately felt on edge. There was something—or someone—on the other side of the door. At first, I thought there was a burglar, but since our doors are always unlocked, they would have immediately stormed in if that were the situation.

I cautiously took a few more steps and stood beside Bella. I looked outside the window by the door and saw what looked to be an eight-year-old girl.

Clad in a school uniform like you'd associate with the 1950s, she appeared eerily pale, like a ghost from the past. When I looked closer at her face, her eyes were black—two round midnight-colored marbles and nothing else. My heart started to race as she knocked again, the sound echoing through the silence.

Since there are two doors at the front entrance, I opened the inside door and asked her what she was doing outside so late. She didn't answer me, but instead asked me if she could come in.

What scared me was the way she asked her question. There was a level of confidence in her tone that shouldn't be there. Typically, if a child is up late at night and in need of assistance, their voice would tremble with nervousness or fear.

But this girl spoke with confidence. Each word felt curated and slipped out as if she had practiced these lines on a hundred doorsteps. I briefly imagined her standing on my neighbors' porches, pressing those thin, pale knuckles against their doors.

I just stared at her for a few seconds before she asked again. This time, she addressed me by my first name, her voice filled with familiarity, when asking her question.

The words tightened around my heart. My name felt dirty coming out of her mouth, like it was being used to mock me. I immediately locked the outside door and shut the inside door, locking it too before going to the door that led to the garage.

Appearances of Black-Eyed Children are fairly common among the supernatural community. People often describe these encounters as eerie and unsettling. Witnesses often report feeling a sense of intense fear or dread in the presence of these beings, even before they noticed their eyes were complete marbles of darkness, devoid of all color. The children's pale skin and lifeless expressions add to the overall feeling of unease.

Witnesses often describe the children's requests to enter homes or vehicles as urgent and persistent, with some feeling an overwhelming compulsion to let them in, despite their instincts telling them otherwise. The stories also mention that these encounters typically occur late at night or in remote locations, adding to the mysterious and sinister nature of these children. While most encounters involve children of normal appearance, there are a few accounts that describe these beings with talon-like feet, further fueling the belief in their supernatural nature.

As I was about to lock it, I heard her voice coming from outside of the garage. She said, "Please let me in, miss. I won't hurt you." I was so terrified by this that I became completely immobile. After a minute, which seemed like hours, I snapped out of this trance and locked the garage door.

I then ran back to my bed and pulled the covers over myself like a frightened child, hearing her knocking every five seconds and asking to come in. My cats were going nuts, hissing at the doors. Bella was growling louder. The animals' growling must have scared this little girl away because she eventually stopped.

Naturally, I didn't sleep at all that night. And I couldn't sleep much for the next few days either, only falling asleep for an hour before waking up in a panic. Whenever I did fall asleep for that one hour, I swear I could hear her voice calling my name, and I could see those black eyes of hers.

Thankfully, I haven't seen or heard from this strange girl since. I had read the stories and knew enough to never, ever let these children into your house. I'm glad I didn't.

I can't imagine what that thing had in store for me.

SOMETHING IN MY HOUSE

A boy's restful sleep is shattered by his little sister. She begs him to follow her. As his eyes adjust to the darkness, he becomes increasingly aware: This is not his sister.

FIELD NOTES

Location: An isolated town in Texas, USA
Date/Time: Just before sunrise, in the space between sleep and wakefulness
Atmosphere: Vulnerable, the feeling of being watched

I live in a little town mostly run by farmers and country folk out in Texas. It's the literal definition of the "middle of nowhere."

Just beyond my backyard is several hundred acres of pasture, and right across my driveway is a few miles of dense woodland. On my property, I often engage in hiking and fishing, and although I've encountered and heard many things, this story stands out. I live with my family, which comprises my parents and my little sister. We live in a little one-story home with a large open-floor living room and kitchen smack dab in the middle of the house.

On one side of the living room is my bedroom. My little sister's is right next to mine. On the opposite side is where my parents' room is. We have our front door in the living room, and the back door in the kitchen, directly opposite one another. In my bedroom, my bed is across the room from my door and in the corner, against the wall.

While lying in bed, I can only see my door out of the corner of my right eye. Our floors are very creaky and loud. It's impossible to sneak around anywhere. One day, I strolled along a path in the woods that my dad had made for us years ago. The entire time we were out there, I felt like I was being watched.

SOMETHING THAT SOUNDED LIKE MY SISTER AND RESEMBLED TWO PEOPLE CLOSE TO ME WAS JUST INSIDE OUR HOUSE TALKING TO ME. ON TOP OF THAT, IT WAS TRYING TO GET ME TO FOLLOW IT OUTSIDE.

My sister felt it too; the woods were way too quiet, so we headed home early. That night, our dogs were going insane. Our array of dogs often engaged in playful running between the front and back doors. But this time, they took it to a whole new level, repeating the sprint endlessly. My dad went outside with a flashlight and walked around the house, but he never found anything. We decided to let our big dogs run outside for the night, something we don't normally do because we were worried someone—or something—was going to try to hurt our outside animals or rob us.

It isn't overly common in our region, but someone had broken into our neighbor's house less than a month before. We didn't want to take any chances, considering we have a lot of expensive ranching equipment and our animals are our babies. The dogs settled down after a while, and everybody went to bed.

In the early morning, around five, before sunrise, someone opened my bedroom door and called my name—awaking me. I was still very much not awake (I take all morning and a cup of coffee to wake up at any time, especially before eight), so my vision was blurry, and I wasn't processing well.

I could hear my dogs going insane outside somewhere, but I didn't realize at that moment that it meant there was something wrong.

My little sister poked her head into my room, not even enough for me to see her neck, and waved at me. She whispered my name repetitively, which only got a hum out of me. "You need to come outside! You must see this. Hurry!"

I wiped my eyes, trying to clear them because my sister, who has dark hair, appeared blonde. The only person I know who's blonde is my best friend, who came over pretty often—but I knew she wasn't spending the night, so I was confused.

This person at my door looked like a combination of my best friend and my little sister. "What are you doing up?" I asked.

My "sister" didn't answer my question.

Instead, she just repeated, "Hurry up! I have to show you what's outside! If you don't come, you're going to miss it." She started to giggle hysterically.

I told her to go away and rolled over. I remember hearing my parents' door open. The girl at my door giggled again, then slammed my door hard enough to shake the wall.

I jumped, nearly falling out of bed, just in time to hear heavy and loud footsteps run straight out the back door. I got up and walked into my kitchen to see my dad standing there.

"Who was in our house just now?" he asked, not even looking at me. I turned to look in my sister's room, but she had just walked out to see what the commotion was about.

Could this be another story about a Skinwalker? With all these stories about them, one has to wonder: Has anyone managed to snap a picture of one? Well, possibly.

In 2014, a disturbing picture of a humanoid figure with elongated limbs circulated on social media. The being's camouflage in the surrounding environment caused concern and fascination. According to the post, the geologist who captured the photo had been conducting routine work in an oil field when he noticed the strange presence. Intrigued, he used a heat signature device to capture further evidence of the entity. The image and the story quickly gained traction, generating widespread discussion and debate about the existence of Skinwalkers and the potential dangers they pose.

Our back door was wide open, the lock completely broken. I could see our dogs tearing after something in the distance. I think that was the moment that it hit me. Something that sounded like my sister and resembled two people close to me was just inside our house talking to me. On top of that, it was trying to get me to follow it outside.

Afterward, we enhanced security at our residence through the installation of alarms, new heavy-duty locks, electric fencing, and surveillance cameras.

A little after this, my sister told me something similar happened to her, but she had seen a taller and darker version of my dad. She said he told her the exact same things to try to lure her outside. Within a month of that, we recorded something on the cameras wandering near our most distant barn.

It was about six feet (2 m) tall, naked, and really pale. The cameras were so blurry that it was hard to distinguish anything else. It scratched around the barn door for a minute before my dogs found it and scared it off.

My dad thought some naked druggie showed up, but like I said, we live in the middle of nowhere. That would be a long walk for anybody, especially a drugged person with no shoes in the cold. I have reason to believe this thing was a Skinwalker that just kept coming back.

Even years after, when I thought I was safe, our cameras picked up something walking across our field in the distance. In the video, it screamed and ran into the woods. I'm scared it has come back.

MALEVOLENT WATERS

During my youth, I swam with my family in a lake in Texas and felt something slippery and rough swim past my leg. I remember when fear overwhelmed me and I lost my ability to swim.

Fear of water encompasses several phobias. Having witnessed the Lovecraftian horrors washed up on beaches or captured on deep-sea cameras, I empathize with those who fear the unpredictable oceans and seemingly calm lakes. Many people are not strong swimmers, making drowning a frightening possibility when we go in the water.

The idea of the abyss can make a swim turn into a panicked race back to shore. It can conjure up the vision of slimy, scaley tendrils reaching up from the watery void to yank you below the surface.

The stories you are about to read evoke our deepest fear: the unknown. And nothing represents the unknown quite as well as dark waters.

EYES EVERYWHERE

Peering over the edge of the boat, all that's visible are the small dots of stars reflected in the water's surface. But when trying to get back to shore, the spots in the water reveal their true form.

FIELD NOTES

Location: Off a Georgian Bay dock, Ontario, Canada
Date/Time: A late night in 2011
Atmosphere: Tranquil, then rocked by palpable desperation

This story takes place in 2011. My family and I had just gone down to Lion's Head, Ontario, Canada, to visit my stepdad's brother and his family. I was at a point in my life where I hated everyone and wanted to be by myself. I was rebellious, and I didn't care if anyone knew. We stayed at a trailer park near the Georgian Bay docks. At the dock, there were boats you could rent.

One night, halfway through the week of our visit, I snuck out—which was difficult to do when we were all in a trailer, but I was determined. I walked to the docks and untied one of the paddle boats left there. Normally, these boats are driven by two people, but I was fine with taking it slow. I got a good distance from the harbor, just enough that I could see it. I took out my phone and plugged in my headphones to listen to my music. It was better to appreciate the stars that we don't get to see in the city.

I lost track of time and was nodding off. I decided to go back. I got up from my resting position and looked around, searching. At first, I was serene, thinking that staying a few more minutes would be fine. But after a few minutes, it dawned on me that I couldn't see the dock anymore. It had to be around there somewhere, but where?

THERE HAD TO BE AT LEAST TWO DOZEN OF THESE EYES SURROUNDING MY SMALL BOAT.

I started to paddle toward the closest landmass I could see. I couldn't have been that far from the harbor, could I? After a few minutes of desperate paddling, I realized something: I wasn't moving. Initially, I thought I was stuck in some weeds or a log or something, so I looked over the edge but I saw nothing.

There were only the stars reflected on the calm water. I rotated around the boat, trying to find whatever I was stuck on. Peering over the left side, I spotted it. At first, I thought it was a large star or even a regular one that was distorted by the water. But it didn't move with the waves like the others. Then I noticed another, and another.

And another.

There had to be at least two dozen of these eyes surrounding my small boat.

Each eye looked to be a few feet (1 m) down and the size of a bowling ball.

Fear petrified me. For a few minutes, I sat there and looked into those eyes—but they didn't move.

For a moment, I thought maybe they were some sort of metal obstruction that was reflecting the light oddly, until one blinked. That one blink shocked me out of my paralyzed state, and I sat back in my seat and pedaled as hard as I could. But no matter what I did, I couldn't move from that spot.

After half an hour, I was tired and gave up. Another idea occurred to me. I opened the compartment in the back, pulled out the emergency kit, and grabbed the flashlight. I tried to illuminate the mysterious object beneath my vessel, but my light revealed nothing but an inky void. Whether it was the skin of whatever that thing was or the darkness of the abyss below, it didn't matter. I had one goal in mind. I threw the flashlight at the eye closest to the boat—and the eye seemed to blink. In fact, all the eyes blinked in unison.

Out of nowhere, something jolted me from my position, leaned over the edge of the boat, and forcefully flung me back into my seat. I didn't care about anything except getting off the lake, so I took the boat to the nearest shore. Unfortunately, that shore was nearly two miles (3 km) from the trailer park. So, I ended up spending the rest of the night in the woods.

When I got back, it was nearly 10 a.m., and my parents had a search party looking for me. I was in a ton of trouble and there was damage to the boat that I had to pay for, but I was just happy to be alive. Still, one thing was on my mind: If the boat had stopped before I realized I was being watched, how long was that thing watching me? And what did it want?

I told my family about it, but no one believed me.

It would just be nice to have some answers.

With this story dipping our toes into the waters of the Great Lakes, it's hard not to talk about Bessie, also known as the Lake Erie Monster.

Theresa Kovach reported seeing this creature in the 1980s, vividly describing Bessie as having a reptilian appearance, resembling a snake with its long, sinuous body. The most striking feature was its enormous flippers, like those of a plesiosaur, a prehistoric aquatic reptile. This suggested that Bessie might be a living relic from a bygone era. The sheer size of the creature left Kovach in awe, as she believed it could easily have overturned a boat with its immense power. However, on that particular day, Bessie seemed to be in a playful mood, as Kovach reported that it was merely frolicking in the gentle waves of Lake Erie.

SOMETHING STARED BACK

A luscious landscape of exotic fish and corals vanishes as a drop-off is reached. Down, down, and down some more, something massive peers up and begins to move.

FIELD NOTES
Location: Too far from the Honduran coast
Date/Time: The perfect time of year for snorkeling and catching some rays
Atmosphere: Relaxed and ready for a vacation

Despite encountering strange and creepy things, my love for the water—especially the ocean—remains unwavering. Not even what happened to me when I was fifteen years old could shake my love.

It started when my mom and I took a cruise down through the Caribbean, stopping at all the well-known destinations along the coast of Mexico and some of the smaller Central American countries.

Our last stop before heading back to port was a tiny island off the coast of Honduras, and we had booked what was supposed to be a relaxing snorkeling excursion. Sure, it isn't the most famous for underwater activities, but there are some absolutely gorgeous reefs in the area. I wanted to be a marine biologist at the time, so it was like heaven for me.

We took a small ferry from the main port to the island we would spend the day on, and after lunch, I headed straight to the water. I remember it was strange that day; it was beautiful outside, but there was almost no one else in the water. I think there was only one other person when I first got in, and I seem to remember noticing that they had left while I was out, leaving the reef all to myself.

THE LAST THING I REMEMBER SEEING WAS AN ENORMOUS EYE OPENING UP, LOOKING DIRECTLY AT ME.

The water was like a dream: not too hot or cold, and sporting tall shelves of reddish coral swarming with tropical fish. I don't know how long I spent just floating around, but it must have been hours. At least I know I came out looking like a freshly cooked lobster by the end.

Anyway, I was floating on my stomach and trying to identify any of the fish I could see, meaning I wasn't paying attention to where I was going.

Suddenly, like someone had flipped a switch, the water got *frigid*.

And in the same instant, I found I had kicked my way over the drop-off point.

The reef came to an end, revealing a rugged outcrop that seemed to vanish into the depths beneath me.

This may not seem scary to those who haven't experienced anything like it, but suddenly finding yourself suspended above a seemingly bottomless void causes a sort of primal terror in you. I froze up, suddenly feeling tiny and out of place. The silence of the water in my ears was deafening.

As I stared down into the abyss, I felt a strong sense of vertigo; and just as I was regaining my senses and ability to move, I saw it.

Something shifted in the murky darkness below me. Something impossibly big.

The last thing I remember seeing was an enormous eye opening up, looking directly at me.

The next thing I knew, I was back on shore, trying desperately to explain what had happened to my probably tipsy mom. When I got to the part about seeing something in the water below me, my voice caught. I didn't want to make myself sound crazy by reporting some giant sea creature, especially since she was already barely paying attention. I never told anyone that part of my story and, to this day, still wonder what it was I could have seen.

Maybe it was some whale or other large creature that had drifted closer than usual to shore. I know it's a cliché, but I know it wasn't my mind playing tricks on me. Whatever it was, I was never able to bring myself to look over the deck of the ship at night for the rest of the trip—too scared I'd see something watching me from the darkness again.

The legends surrounding the Lusca are deeply rooted in the folklore of the Bahamas and the Caribbean. Locals believe that this fearsome creature inhabits the mysterious underwater caves known as blue holes, which are found throughout the region. Locals say that the Lusca, a formidable predator, can attack both on land and in the water.

Its half-shark, half-octopus appearance adds to its menacing reputation, instilling fear in those who have heard the tales. Fishermen and scuba divers have reported encounters with the Lusca, recounting terrifying experiences of being pursued or attacked by this hybrid monster. The creature's massive size and powerful tentacles make it a formidable adversary, causing panic and distress among those who venture near its lair. The Lusca's alleged ability to create tidal currents in the inland blue holes further adds to its mystique, with locals attributing the phenomenon to the creature's breathing. Despite questioning from skeptics and scientists, the eyewitness accounts of the Lusca's deadly attacks on unsuspecting individuals have persisted, solidifying its status as a legendary and feared creature of the deep.

FROM THE DARKNESS AT SEA

Far off a restless coastline, a dim light grows stronger
under the waters. It wrenches its observers with fear as the light
moves ever closer, revealing its genuine horror.

FIELD NOTES

Location: Rockaway Beach, New York, USA
Date/Time: A late summer's day in 2018
Atmosphere: A hazy feeling, as a soft and mysterious glow pierces the night

I am an avid believer in the paranormal and have had many experiences. But what I experienced in the summer of 2018 has stuck with me. I went on a late-night trip to Rockaway Beach with a friend, whom I'll refer to as Jay. There's just something magical about having the beach to yourself, with no throngs of humans around. You can enjoy the majesty of the sea under a soft blanket of meditative darkness.

It must have been at least after 10 p.m. when Jay and I got there and found parking. There were very few people around on the boardwalk. We walked until we could get onto the actual beach, since it's sectioned off at many points. As we removed our shoes, our feet were welcomed by the cool sand on a ramp-like walkway leading to the water.

Before laying out the blanket I had brought with me, we found a secluded spot that was not too far from the path leading back. We sat near the water's edge where we could listen to the song of the sea as the waves rolled in and on the shore and got to talking about life.

We spent a considerable amount of time conversing and gazing out toward the horizon and sea, which appeared almost inseparable and merged into an abyss. During nighttime, the ocean appears intensely black, resembling ink, while the sky takes on a subtle shade of navy or deep purple.

There was no moon, and it was cloudy. Additionally, there were no other sources of light nearby due to the dimly lit boardwalk and our considerable distance from any light source. As we sat talking, our voices carried off into that void by the cool sea breeze, barely a whisper above the roar of the restless waves, I saw something peculiar on the horizon.

It was an extremely bright orb of light—so much so it looked like it could have been a star in the ocean. I found it odd, as it was so luminous and just appeared out of nowhere. I mentioned this to Jay, and he noted it as well, but we continued to talk as I watched it, now focused on the only light out on the water.

Slowly, this light crept toward the shore, lingering on the water. I don't recall seeing it bob or meander with the waves too much, but it moved steadily. I had my eyes on it the entire time and when it got nearly halfway to shore, it vanished.

The sea returned to its familiar, boundless darkness. But I couldn't help but feel perplexed by how something so radiant could vanish so suddenly beneath the waves, without any indication of sinking or fading, as if it were being extinguished. When that happened, it made me wonder if I had really seen anything, and if I had, what had it been?

Shortly after, I witnessed the reappearance of the same light; but this time, it was much nearer. Instead of moving at a right angle to the shoreline like before, it appeared to have a sense of purpose and moved diagonally, almost in parallel, to the shore. Surprisingly, it showed no signs of being influenced by the tide and seemed to move even faster than previously observed.

It was very close to us now, maybe twenty to thirty feet (6 to 9 m) out before it dipped under the water again and vanished without a trace. An unmistakable and

WHEN THAT HAPPENED, IT MADE ME WONDER IF I HAD REALLY SEEN ANYTHING, AND IF I HAD, WHAT HAD IT BEEN?

The annual death toll from diving accidents in North America is approximately one hundred, and an additional one hundred people lose their lives while diving in other parts of the world. However, the sport of diving is becoming safer thanks to advancements in technology.

The first diving suits were created in the 1710s, and in 1715, John Lethbridge, an English inventor, developed the first completely sealed suit. It included waterproof sleeves, a barrel filled with pressurized air, and a viewing window. People have made continuous improvements since then. We have lost many lives during the process of making improvements, however. Imagine heavy copper helmets dragging their occupants to murky depths to rest for years—possibly until the restless spirit rises from the waters, in search of the land they never found in life.

insurmountable feeling of dread washed over us. We weren't sure why we felt that way, but we couldn't shake the feeling at all.

Thinking about it now makes me shudder. A feeling like that is not something you feel often, but when you do, it's like your senses are screaming at you to flee, your pulse and respiration quicken, and you enter that instinctual and primordial place of fight or flight. However, despite that feeling, we stayed put to see what would play out, as we were both curious.

Suddenly, an object emerged silently from the water on our right side, creating no noticeable ripples apart from the ones caused by the tide. It appeared to be around ten to fifteen feet (3 to 5 m) tall. Jay and I had stopped talking at this point, as we both felt very uncomfortable and seemed to hold our breaths to remain quiet.

I couldn't make out very clear features as I was afraid to even really look at the thing, but Jay and I got this sense: It was aware of us and it knew we were aware of it, as well.

Jay didn't have his glasses on, but from what he could discern, it was bipedal, tall, and looming. Its whole body had a sickly, ghastly yellow hue that seemed to emit a faint glow, reminiscent of light in fog. The closest comparison to its appearance would be that of a ghostly deep-sea diver from a bygone era.

"Do you want to stay?" Jay asked me quietly after a few moments.

"No, let's go. I don't want to be like those people in the horror movies," I said. I knew we were both freaked out; every cell in our bodies was nudging us away.

I quickly picked up my blanket, and we grabbed our shoes and hurried back—avoiding running, as that thing might have perceived it as a challenge or invitation for a chase. It was a little distance down from us and I was glad we sat somewhere that wasn't too far from the trail leading back up to the boardwalk. There was a young woman hanging out by a lifeguard chair near the ramp and Jay asked me if I wanted to ask her if she could see it too. I nodded.

"Excuse me." I tried to keep my voice even. "We're sorry to bother you, but can you see anything down there?" I pointed in the direction we came. I don't remember seeing anything when I looked back and felt concerned about this.

"No, I don't see anything. Why?" the girl replied, her gaze fixated on the horizon, curious to discover any noteworthy sights.

"Oh, well, we thought we saw something weird just now, but it doesn't seem like it's there anymore. Sorry to bother you," I responded, looking back again to where we saw that thing, only to see a deserted beach.

"Be careful and stay safe," Jay said to the girl as we walked past her and up the ramp.

If there are ghosts walking on the seafloor, then there must be a boat or ship to have ferried them. There are plenty of ships that are said to be haunted. Perhaps the most famous is the Flying Dutchman of old European maritime lore.

The most well-known version of the legend revolves around the ship's cursed captain, Hendrick Van der Decken. In a moment of foolishness, he boldly chose to sail through the dangerous waters near the Cape of Good Hope in the midst of a fierce storm, defying even the gods. The ship and its crew are sentenced to sail the seas forever as punishment for their audacity, never to find peace or redemption.

As we returned to the boardwalk, I took a quick glance back toward the spot where we had spotted the mysterious figure. I'm not sure if it was a trick of the lighting, but I could have sworn I glimpsed faint yellow glimmers, similar to the ghostly hue of whatever we had witnessed standing in the water near our previous location. It appeared to exist in a state between reality and illusion, with certain parts of its body faded while others faintly glowed.

It appeared it was lost in thought, fixated on the sand. However, when I caught its eye, it subtly turned its head toward me. Its glow grew stronger.

I twisted my head and didn't look back after that. Jay and I got to the safety of his car before we looked at each other in disbelief.

"Did you see that?" I asked him hesitantly.

"Yes. I can't make any sense of what we just saw," Jay responded.

"Me neither. Did you have a feeling of intense dread before that thing arrived?"

"Without a doubt. It's not as if we both had the same imagination and suddenly felt the same way." His words were heavy, like he was trying to process his thoughts. "A feeling surged through me, as if a billion delicate prods were gently nudging my joints and nerves, whispering, 'Take it slow, take it slow, you need to move.'"

"That would be crazy," I said as I trailed off. We discussed every moment of what just happened some more, but came to no real conclusion.

Jay drove me back to my house and I couldn't shake the feeling that that thing was still thinking of us or searching for us. I felt terrified even when I got to my house and got inside. The situation left Jay feeling shaken as well. I tried to do some research on my phone about this being but I couldn't find anything conclusive.

I never thought I'd see or experience something like that where I live, but it just goes to show you not to take anything for granted and that this world we live in is much stranger than we may ever know.

Never ignore your feelings, especially feelings of dread.

DARK ROADS

There's something ironic about dark roads. Roads are meant to guide you safely to your destination.

Why does a path become ominous after nightfall, even though its purpose is to connect people through the wilderness? Maybe it's the encroaching forests and isolation of traveling between two centers of civilization. Maybe you just can't help but wonder what might burst from the wilds on either side of the road and derail your trip and your mind, all at the same time.

Avoid traveling alone and bring a bright light. Refrain from running out of fuel and do not stop for hitchhikers with chainsaws or claws. Keep these stories in mind as you make your way along the road to reach the other side in one piece.

If you are not ready, your car could become stranded, with the driver missing and only an open door and a trail leading into the nearby foliage serving as clues.

THE BLACK DOG

Trucks barrel down the highway night and day; stories pass
from one trucker to another. And when a warning falls on deaf ears,
the Black Dog is anything but man's best friend.

FIELD NOTES

Location: The vast American highways
Date/Time: The dead of night, around 2021
Atmosphere: The somberness of a lonely night, with a hint of superstitious paranoia

I've been driving a truck for only a short time, but I've always enjoyed hearing stories from the old-timers about the trucking industry's golden age. I've gotten to hear the good, the bad—and as I got into it myself, the superstition.

Everyone, no matter who they run for, where they drive, or how long they've been in it, has seen their share of it. I've witnessed pileups in the winter, vehicle fires in the summer, and beaten the coroner to a wreck once or twice. It's just the nature of the job—the more you're on the road, the more likely you're going to come across unpleasant things. This incident, or what I believe it to be at least, still gets to me on some of the longer nights.

I started driving a truck in 2021. I lost my job at the factory after five years, with no reopening date. I observed truckers working and concluded I could have a job through anything. I went to a small school, got my CDL (commercial driver's license), and joined a trucking company.

After about a year, my buddy asked about driving, so I talked to him, and we got him into a company that would train him and put him on the road. Let's call him Steve.

In British folklore, the Black Dog is often described as a large, spectral canine with glowing red eyes and shaggy fur. People believe it roams the countryside, especially at night, and is often associated with crossroads, graveyards, and ancient burial grounds. The Black Dog is believed to be a harbinger of death or misfortune, with sightings of it being seen as a bad omen. However, there are also tales of the Black Dog appearing to lost travelers and guiding them to safety, suggesting a more benevolent nature.

These contradictory depictions have led to a wide range of interpretations and beliefs surrounding the Black Dog. Some legends even state that the Black Dog will cause an untimely demise for those who encounter it three times, while others believe that certain rituals or charms can appease or ward off the creature. The association of the Black Dog with guarding treasure stems from its connection to certain haunted locations or ancient sites said to be hiding valuable riches. Overall, the Black Dog remains an enigmatic figure in folklore, embodying both fear and protection, darkness and light.

Steve was a few years older than I, in the National Guard reserve, and looking for some work between deployments. He'd been in for a few years, messed up his knee on a training op, and was looking to switch his enlisted job. While all the paperwork was in red tape limbo, he wanted to drive.

I ran flatbed in the Northeast, and he ran box for a super-carrier in Pennsylvania and out West. He even sent me pics of the world's largest truck stop, off Route 80 in Iowa. Our paths rarely crossed on the blacktop, but sometimes we returned to town for downtime. We'd meet up, have a few drinks, and swap stories.

Now, we'd watch scary movies and tell folk tales in the past around campfires, but never got too much into it. One night, we were at my house catching up when he sat back in his chair and said, "Hey, have you ever seen the Black Dog?"

This made me choke on my drink. Most drivers, we've all heard different things about the Black Dog. Some say it brings death, others say it warns you beforehand. You're always tired, but if you're too tired and riding the rumble strip too much, you may see the dog.

So, I sat back and told him my story about it.

"First time, it's a warning. You're tired, get off the road and get some sleep.

"Second time, it'll make you stop. You'll experience something that'll get you to pull over. Animals on the road, mechanical mishaps, random traffic stop by police or DOT (Department of Transportation).

"If you continue, however, and get back between the highway lines, it gets a little foggy from there. No way to know for sure what happens exactly because, from what I've been told, your time is up. Some guys wreck, don't survive. Some end up dead in their rig in the following days. Heart attack, exhaust leaks, the works.

"I've seen it once. Foggy night, Route 84 through New York, February. I was dead tired. Coffee, energy drinks, Marlboros, nothing was working. I took my eyes off the road for a second to fiddle with the radio, and when I looked up, I saw it.

"Through the fog, something skittered off the shoulder and into my lane.

"A shadow.

"It paused to look directly at me. A black, wispy canine shape, with hollow yellowish eyes.

"I shot upright in my seat. With a flatbed, you can't slam on the brakes, or your load will come up to visit you in the cab. And with trucks, you can't swerve much, or you'll roll. So, I just gripped the wheel and braced for an impact, but it didn't come. I passed through where the figure was and kept rolling, pulling off on the shoulder as soon as I could.

"When I got out, I went around the front of my truck to look for damage, fur, blood, anything.

"There was no scratch, nothing. I stood there in shock for a few minutes before recalling the stories I had heard. After connecting the dots, I realized what I had encountered. So, I climbed back in the seat, pulled off at the next off-ramp, and got some much-needed sleep.

"I ended up being late for my delivery, but I'm still around."

As I fidgeted in my chair and took another sip, feeling the liquid warm my throat, he chuckled and said, "I've actually seen it twice now."

THE BLACK DOG

MOST DRIVERS, WE'VE ALL HEARD DIFFERENT THINGS ABOUT THE BLACK DOG. SOME SAY IT BRINGS DEATH, OTHERS SAY IT WARNS YOU BEFOREHAND.

I raised an eyebrow, and he continued.

"Yeah. Last week, while heading east toward Ohio, I saw it once alongside the road. Now, I was far from my delivery, so I just kept going." He stopped sipping his coffee before continuing. "About two hours later, I thought I saw it again, but it ended up being a deer that shot into the road as I went to pass it. I ended up hitting the darn thing. I pulled off to check and thankfully it just busted some plastics."

Despite my growing nervousness, I maintained a calm demeanor as he sat across from me in my living room. I said, "Well, what happened?"

"I finished my run and ended up delivering. Caught some rest and started again."

We both kind of laughed it off; such is the industry. We finished our drinks and chatted into the early a.m. before hitting the hay.

A week or so later, I got a call from Steve. He got into some argument with his dispatch over getting home in time for a wedding, so he ended up quitting. He seemed a little angry about it, but nothing serious.

Over the next week or so, his luck just kept getting worse. The motor blew in his car, work problems, money, relationships—the works.

Two days into vacation, I got another call from a different friend. Steve used the proverbial self-checkout line. Left a note, but none of us got the specifics. The Army did their own investigation; never heard from that either.

It's been almost a year since, and I'll be the first to admit it may all be a really bad coincidence. But I am damn scared to see that dog again.

To everyone reading, and my fellow drivers, be safe.

And to Steve: I miss you, brother.

STINKER IN THE FIELDS

Nerves are on edge walking home. The wind tugs at the skin as
an odor, like an omen, wafts in. The air is thick with the stench of death as
the cold wind cuts through, accompanied by the sight of a lumbering
figure on the roadside. It is not only the cold that bites.

FIELD NOTES

Location: An undisclosed location in the UK
Date/Time: The dead of night, September 2002
Atmosphere: Eerie foreboding and otherworldly silence

The following story takes place in September 2002, just after the release of the movie
Signs in movie theaters in the UK. At the time, I was a relatively poor student whose only
"real" expense was a monthly subscription membership to the local cinema, allowing
me to watch unlimited movies as often as I wanted—provided there were showings and
seats available, of course.

Not a bad deal. I used that membership regularly. With my university housemates
off visiting family, I found myself with nothing to do on that fateful night. So, I made the
spontaneous decision to go and watch the midnight showing of *Signs*. Yeah, I know. Already,
I'm raising typical horror trope red flags—seeing a somewhat creepy movie at midnight.

Regardless, I took what little spare cash I had, went to see the movie, and foolishly
spent the money I should have saved for the taxi fare on treating myself to some decent
food and drink to enjoy the movie. It was more appetizing than the sorry half-empty
bottle of Dr. Pepper and the cheap bag of sweets I had smuggled in. So, when the movie
ended and people were shuffling out to go home just after 2 a.m., I had no other option
but to walk home.

From one dangerous canine to the next. According to northern English folklore, a werewolf-human hybrid called Old Stinker has been terrorizing the villagers for centuries, appearing during full moons and causing fear and havoc. The authorities took the reports seriously due to growing eyewitness accounts and the genuine fear expressed by the residents. Newspapers published chilling stories of encounters with Old Stinker, with witnesses hearing bone-chilling howls and seeing a large figure in the shadows. The authorities launched investigations and the community took precautions, arming themselves with silver bullets and staying indoors after sunset. Paranormal experts and werewolf enthusiasts came to Hull, located in the north of England, to capture evidence of Old Stinker, adding to the excitement and terror in the city.

Now, being younger and significantly more foolish, I didn't really think much of this. I didn't consider that a three-mile (5 km) walk through dimly lit, deserted roads past vast fields in the chilly silence of the midnight hour would pose any danger to me. I knew roughly where I was going. It was a simple, straight-line route that I had gone through by car or bus several times, so I didn't consider it much of an issue. More red flags, I know. At this point, pretty much every horror movie protagonist has sealed their fate.

I set off, embarking down the footpath onto the long road, where it and the pavement disappeared—leaving only a vast expanse of untamed, grassy verge that led to ditches. These ditches bordered a densely populated wooded area and several vacant fields.

As I strolled down the road, feeling the fresh chill in the air, my mind was filled with creepy thoughts, imagining the worst and recalling scenes from the movie. You see, the area I live in is something of a hotspot for strange activities, including UFO sightings, and if you've seen *Signs*, you'll know why my mind was doing its best to freak me out. But thankfully, as I walked down the long stretch of road, there were no extraterrestrial sights.

But there was something else. Generally, the early morning hours are quiet, with only occasional sounds from owls, foxes, cats, or dogs in nearby urban areas. And as I was walking past a significantly wooded area, past several ditches and fields, I was expecting to hear the soft skittering of smaller animals. But after about ten minutes, I realized I was hearing nothing. No hoots, no yips or growls, no snorts.

Nothing.

I came to a halt, taking in my surroundings, shivering from the biting cold. It felt off. Intimidating, even. After a few moments, I heard something, a strange shuffling sound in the field just across the road from me. The sound of crop stems crunching, like they were being trodden over by something big. But there was no one else around. Not a car on the road, not a person in the area—just dim streetlights and a long stretch of nothing.

Despite feeling uneasy, I pressed on, aware that I must be nearing the gym, the only landmark signaling a change in direction and the beginning of another lengthy road toward civilization. I held hope that whatever I had heard would be content to stay behind in the fields. Maybe it was a deer. Maybe it was some unseen barnyard critter that I couldn't make out in the dark.

But as I continued, the sounds of crunching and shuffling echoed beside me, creating an eerie atmosphere. It was still quiet. Still cold. At this point, I quickened my pace, hoping that whatever was following me would stay in the fields, fenced off by chicken wire, barbed wire, and electric fences.

But after a few moments, the sounds continued, picking up the pace themselves. Now, I know it wasn't me. I wasn't hearing an echo of myself; I was walking in sneakers on a damp, grassy verge. Nothing was going to crunch that loudly. And I certainly wasn't that heavy.

I paused, looking about, glancing toward the fields as I slowly kept walking along the verge on the opposite side of the road. It was then that I saw it. My initial sighting is best described as a large, black shape moving along the edge of the field. I couldn't quite see it. I didn't really have anything to provide light, and mobile phones back then were dimly lit green screens at best. So, I was catching

AT THIS POINT, I QUICKENED MY PACE, HOPING THAT WHATEVER WAS FOLLOWING ME WOULD STAY IN THE FIELDS, FENCED OFF BY CHICKEN WIRE, BARBED WIRE, AND ELECTRIC FENCES.

fleeting glances between the overlapping streetlights. It moved along the edge, in the same direction as me.

I couldn't make out what it was at that moment. Only that it was big and moving in the same direction as me. With a nervous swallow, I decided to turn and sprint. I just needed to get to the gym. From there, it was civilization. There would be an abundance of light, other people—drunks, even—but as I sprinted, as my heart raced, I heard it shuffling and snapping beside me.

A wire fence shook and rattled as something climbed straight over it, as though it were no obstacle. As I ran, I heard the sounds across the road from me, where the fields were disappearing to another ditch: another grassy verge with hedgerows and small bushes as a backdrop as we got to housing areas.

Then, a noxious odor assaulted my senses. It was a rancid smell carried by the wind as it swept toward me. I retched and staggered, finally coming to a halt near the walls of the gym.

From there, I gazed across the way, and the source of the stench became more evident. A massive dark form with scruffy fur, yet unmistakably resembling a dog. It loped along, going from all fours to upright and back to four at its own whim. And I could hear it panting and sniffing as it looked toward me with gold-red eyes.

One thought came to mind when I saw this: werewolf. It really looked like the stereotypical wolfman.

But it was also at that point I realized that I was in trouble. I was utterly exhausted, completely drained. I was in a cold sweat, and this thing was slowly approaching me. But I made it to the junction I needed to get to. Crossing the road brought me to built-up areas where I could follow a footbridge to some houses, then

The Beast of Gévaudan was a ferocious predator that terrorized the rural region of what was called Gévaudan in Southern France during the mid-eighteenth century.

The attacks were characterized by their brutality, with victims being mauled and torn apart. The creature was described as a wolflike beast, larger than any known wolf, with a reddish-brown coat, a wide chest, and enormous jaws. It possessed remarkable agility and strength, able to leap great distances and carry off victims weighing up to one hundred pounds (45 kg). Despite efforts by the local community and the French monarchy to hunt down the creature, it managed to elude capture, leaving behind a trail of fear and devastation. Many theories emerged regarding the identity of the Beast, ranging from a large wolf or wolf-dog hybrid to a supernatural entity or mythical creature. The mystery of the Beast of Gévaudan endures to this day.

down the main road to home. Hoping for light or something to deter the thing following me, I crossed the road with determination.

Fortunately, this was the moment when luck would be on my side. I didn't pay attention, so I did not see a lorry (a truck, for American readers) driving fairly slowly at night, coming by the roundabout. Thankfully, the driver wasn't going too fast, so seeing an exhausted guy slowly making his way across the road, the driver was able to stop in time.

The lorry stopped, the driver leaning out to shout profanities at me. I looked toward him, trying to apologize—and then, a shiver ran down my spine. The creature was approaching behind the lorry. But as the driver continued to shout, it seemed the creature was put off. There was a loud *thunk* that rang out as it jumped up onto the back of the lorry, causing the driver to stop and look at me.

"Hey, do you see that?" The driver asked me.

"Y-yeah . . . I see it." My mouth could barely form a coherent response, the words feeling heavy on my tongue. I couldn't describe it.

I was shaken, my heart pounding as I watched the driver struggle to peer around the cab, desperate to see what was on the roof of the trailer.

We both watched whatever it was hobble along the trailer before jumping down past the driver, between myself and the lorry. It looked at me one last time, then darted off toward the ditch, toward the river—and more importantly, the local drain.

The lorry driver and I looked at each other, shaking our heads. We both agreed: probably a big, stray dog. But both of us knew what we saw wasn't right. The rest of my trip home was uneventful. I got in just past 3:30 a.m. and clambered up the stairs to my room to collapse and sleep the following day away. I kept this to myself, knowing that the circumstances were filled with numerous warning signs that no one would take seriously.

Some twenty years later, I embraced my old love of the paranormal and did local research out of curiosity. I think I may have found what I saw that day.

People have been spotting Old Stinker, Hull's local werewolf, for a number of decades. Its name comes from the rotting and sulfurous stench of its breath. It's been spotted along the industrial estates, particularly along the Barnston drain, which was fairly close to the route I had taken that night.

Old Stinker had hunted me. Stalked me in the frosty night and I only escaped because of circumstantial luck. It probably assumed that targeting a single student would be simple, but the addition of a roaring lorry and an angry, shouting man changed the situation entirely. And for that, I am thankful.

I will say that, since that encounter, I have made a point not to walk long distances in the middle of the night through lonely back roads. It's a different experience stumbling back from a late night out through crowded areas where CCTV cameras are ubiquitous and people are always present, than it is to walk back in complete silence with dim lighting, no surveillance, and the possibility of encountering only sheep or ponies.

ENCOUNTER ON THE ROAD

A father struggles to remain calm while fighting with something—or someone—outside his truck. A boy awakens and feels horrified as he sees exactly what that "something" is.

FIELD NOTES

Location: Southeastern USA
Date/Time: The summer of 2005, just after the end of the school year
Atmosphere: A tranquil, yet slightly unsettling, open road

This story happened to me when I was about eight years old. My dad was a trucker, and as expected, he spent a lot of time on the road. Whenever I was on break from school, my dad would often take me with him trucking across many states. I thoroughly enjoyed going with him, especially because the open road provided a sense of tranquility. Plus, we made frequent stops to indulge in delicious meals.

This incident occurred during the summer of 2005, a week after the school year had ended. My dad told me to pack a bit extra this time because he was going farther than usual on his route. That evening, I started packing my clothes and any sort of entertainment, which ended up being my Game Boy Color.

Early the next morning, my dad and I left for the place where the truck was kept, and we set off from there. The first couple of hours were usually just driving nonstop, so I took the time to play my Game Boy and gaze out the window from time to time. About three hours into the trip, my dad asked me if I was hungry; we went to a McDonald's for some food. After we finished our meals, we got back in the truck and began driving again.

About an hour later, a jarring, scraping sound echoed from the bottom right side of the truck. My dad pulled over and exited the truck to see what the noise was. I stayed inside, so I didn't see what happened, but I remember my dad was on the phone and he sounded upset. My dad eventually got back inside the truck and told me we were going to have to stop by somewhere first because something had happened to the truck.

We arrived at a repair shop, and my dad went to talk to someone who was inside. Just a couple of minutes later, my dad hurried back and instructed me to exit the truck as it required inspection. I was never told what the problem with the truck was. My dad and I waited for about four more hours for the man to finish what he was doing, and once he was done, we left and continued.

It was about 6 p.m. at this time, and I was still playing on my Game Boy because there was still light out. The original Game Boy didn't have back lighting, and I wanted to play as long as I could before the sun set. I continued to play for another hour or so before getting very sleepy. I turned my Game Boy off and rested my head on the side of the door, staring out the window and watching the trees as we drove by, eventually falling asleep.

Abruptly, I snapped out of my sleep as my dad sped down the road, causing the truck to vibrate beneath me. I remember looking out the window and seeing that the sun had already started setting. My dad told me, "Don't be scared," which confused me because I had no idea what was going on. I questioned my dad about his fast driving, but he remained silent and focused on the road ahead. I stared at him—and that's when I saw movement coming from outside his window.

Initially, I only saw something white quickly approaching and then retreating from his window. I was still very confused, wondering what the heck I was seeing and why it was going so fast. The object then came into view again, and this time got close enough to slap the driver's side window. When it got that close to the truck, I was able to get a pretty good look at it.

There, out the window, was a lady with long, black hair cascading over her face, dressed in a flowing white gown, effortlessly floating. She flew back, retreating for a moment, then swiftly returned and forcefully slapped against the window before flying away again. This thing then came back, and I quickly closed my eyes as I saw it was about to press its face against the driver's side window.

There are countless stories of spirits haunting the roadside. Phantoms caught lurking through trees as cars rush by. Hitchhikers who vanish before they reach their destination. And if you're looking for a horrific encounter with the apparition of a ghastly woman, look no further than Bloody Bride Bridge in Stevens Point, Wisconsin, USA.

The legend of Bloody Bride Bridge has been passed down for generations in the Stevens Point area. According to the local lore, the Bride was on her way to her wedding when she lost control of her car on the treacherous curves of Highway 66 and met her untimely demise. Ever since that fateful day, drivers have reported chilling encounters with her ghostly presence. Some people say they've seen her ghostly form sitting in the back seat of their car, wearing a wedding gown stained with blood. Others have seen her sorrowful and longing gaze in the rearview mirror. These spine-tingling encounters have become a cautionary tale for those who dare to drive along this desolate stretch of road at night.

I heard my dad scream and curse and tell me not to look. I kept my eyes shut and I heard my dad whimper. All I can remember after that is that I kept my eyes closed until we got to civilization.

Whatever we saw that night haunts me even to this day. I have no idea what that thing was and what it wanted. I don't know exactly which state we were in when it took place, only that it was somewhere in the Southeast USA.

This was never talked about between my dad and me. He passed away six years ago, and until recently, I thought that he never told anyone about what happened. However, my mom and I were talking about my dad and his side of the family, and we eventually started talking about my grandparents. As we were talking about my grandmother, my mom—seemingly out of nowhere—asked me about that night when my dad and I were out trucking.

I was shocked to discover that my dad had informed my mom about it, considering they had never mentioned it before.

THERE, OUT THE WINDOW, WAS A LADY WITH LONG, BLACK HAIR CASCADING OVER HER FACE, DRESSED IN A FLOWING WHITE GOWN, EFFORTLESSLY FLOATING.

She asked me if I saw the face of the thing that was outside the truck and I said no.

She stayed silent for a couple of seconds and then asked me if I ever noticed my dad acting weird after that. I told her that the only thing I found strange was that he never talked about it.

My mom then told me the scariest thing I ever heard.

She explained to me that when the thing pressed its face against the driver's side window, it said something to my dad.

It said something to him in my grandma's voice.

His mom's voice.

When he heard that voice, he turned to see the thing's face, and his heart sank as he recognized the unmistakable features of his deceased mother.

According to my mom, that experience forever haunted my dad, and he would have constant nightmares because of it.

THE BEAST AT THE WINDOW

A car is parked on the side of the road, its occupant
catching some needed sleep during a long drive. Danger lurks outside
the passenger-side window, waiting for a way inside.

FIELD NOTES

Location: On the road toward home and family, anywhere
Date/Time: The witching hour
Atmosphere: The feeling of something being very wrong,
yet no one is around to help

This story happened to me when I was twenty-eight years old.

It all started when I was driving home from the north of the state, trying to get down south back to my family. A four- to five-hour drive was really taking it out of me, and I needed to catch up on sleep. I pulled onto the side of the road. Since I hadn't seen many cars, I decided a few hours of sleep wouldn't hurt. I soon found myself dozing off to the silence in the truck, waking up around 3 a.m. Something had been "hitting" something else in the nearby forest. It sounded like someone beating a steel bat against a tree.

It really unsettled me because I had never heard such strange noises from animals before, despite my experience with hunting and encountering various wildlife. I attempted to fall back asleep, but woke up about an hour later, suddenly jolted awake by something hitting my car door. I felt the entire car shake and nearly had a heart attack.

While surveying the area, I couldn't ignore the sight of breath outside my passenger-side window turning into visible fog—a common occurrence in cold conditions.

This fog was rising every few seconds. It seemed like someone, or something, was on the other side. Me being paranoid, I tried to lower myself in my seat. Now, with my body

When someone transforms into a werewolf, not only do their physical features change, but their body also undergoes a painful metamorphosis. As their transformation progresses, the flats of their feet elongate excruciatingly, adapting to their new lupine form. The bones and ligaments stretch and reshape, causing intense discomfort during the process. The creature's knees appear to be inverted when viewed from a distance as it flees, creating a deceptive illusion of articulation. This peculiar visual effect, combined with the creature's swift movements, may confuse witnesses and add to the mystique surrounding these legendary beings.

flattened on the seat, I could see something looking in. I didn't know if it had seen me, but it was drooling.

It appeared to be the head of a wolf. Its muzzle pressed hard against the window, covering it in smudged saliva. This animal was panting heavily, as if it had sprinted for miles to reach my car, and it trembled as if it were angry at me. Not the kind of "scared" shaking, but the "I want to beat you to death" kind of shaking. I guess it hadn't seen me because it soon left.

I got up, watching it walk back into the woods, shocked to see it was walking on only two legs. These legs were not the legs of a wolf or a man but bent backward like those of a deer or an elk.

Had it not been for the moonlight, I wouldn't have been able to see it. After it was far gone, I sped off back home, quivering the entire way. When I got home, I ran in, locked the doors, grabbed my .45 handgun, and hunkered down for the night. I kept my gun close.

The next morning, I saw that my car had a huge dent in the side, like that thing had thrown a bowling ball at it with full force. I couldn't open the car door on the passenger side because it was completely totaled. I don't know what it was, but I've learned to never go down that road again.

SWITCHING SEATS IN THE DARK

With a late night looming, eyes grow heavy and fingers become loose. With the car pulled over, there's nothing to be seen. Only darkness surrounds the vehicle. Could that be why something managed to sneak right up to the window?

FIELD NOTES

Location: On the way home, anywhere
Date/Time: Around 2012, when you're the only one on the road
Atmosphere: Tiredness and fatigue changing into fear and panic

I can still feel the chills running down my spine when I think about the incident that happened around eight or nine years ago.

I am a female, and I was twenty-four at the time this happened. My family lived about an hour out of town, and cell reception was sketchy at best. Most of the time, you couldn't get reception at all. I am a bit of a nervous person, so not having cell reception already put me on edge.

I always hated having to drive home in the dark. I feared breaking down in the middle of nowhere. And because we lived so far out of town, the lighting on the road was scarce.

My mom was the one who drove most of the time because I only had a permit and only drove at night when necessary. It may seem weird for me to have only had a permit at that age, but medical problems made it so I wasn't able to learn to drive before then. (I still can't drive due to injury, but that's another story.)

This story begins when my mom and I were driving home late one night after a long day in town. We were about thirty minutes from home, so we had already been out of

MY MOM TOOK A QUICK LOOK AROUND AND GOT IN ON HER SIDE, BUT AS SHE WAS SHUTTING THE DOOR, SOMETHING PULLED ON IT.

reception for a while. My mom didn't get a lot of sleep the night before, but she was the one driving because of my inexperience with driving at night.

As fatigue overcame her, she drifted off in the driver's seat. Usually, I could just talk to her to keep her awake. Eventually, my mom got tired enough that talking no longer worked, and she started to swerve into the wrong lane. I yelled, and she woke up. But I was still having a lot of trouble keeping her awake.

I suggested I should drive the rest of the way. She agreed. Both of us were on edge, feeling uneasy about being in an area with no cell reception and the need to change seats, which would require stepping out of the car into darkness surrounded by dense woods.

Realizing we were left with no alternatives, we came across a vast open space a couple of miles away, far from any trees. This reassured me that we would have sufficient time to flee if anyone or anything emerged from the trees.

We stopped and got out of the car. For some reason, I felt unusually comfortable and didn't hurry like I usually did when it was dark. I got in the driver's side and shut the door. In this car, all doors had to be all the way shut or none of the doors would lock. My mom took a quick look around and got in on her side, but as she was shutting the door, something pulled on it.

I couldn't lock the doors because her door wasn't closed all the way. I couldn't figure out what to do. Suddenly, she screamed at me to drive. It felt like I couldn't get out of there fast enough. I must have been going seventy (113 kph) on a fifty-mile-per-hour (80 kph) road for about two miles (3 km) before I finally felt safe enough to stop in the middle of the road just long enough for my mom to shut her door.

I also suddenly thought about the fact that my window had been down, and it terrifies me to think what would have happened if it had come to my window. The scariest part is that the nearest trees or bushes for hiding in were at least three hundred feet (91 m) away. I am pretty sure there is no human or animal of any kind that can get to the car in what had to be less than a second, and whatever it was had to have had hands to be pulling on the door. To this day, I am not sure what wanted to get in our car or what would have happened if it had.

I don't feel that whatever we encountered out there that night was human.

Although this narrator didn't provide us with much information, there are many American rumors and folklore about the unexplained lurking on the roadside.

Dating back to 1936, the Beast of Bray Road is described as a hairy humanoid creature with canine characteristics, often sighted on rural roads in Wisconsin. Another is the Bunny Man legend from northern Virginia, which states that a figure dressed in a white rabbit costume appears at midnight on Halloween. If his name is spoken three times, he will harm those present.

THE GHOST ON I-4

What was meant to be a fun night out cruising in a sports car after a few drinks turns grim. The sight of a peculiar face on the highway causes the car to come to an immediate halt, compelling the driver to step out.

FIELD NOTES

Location: Plant City, Florida, USA, on the I-4
Date/Time: A Friday night in the early years of the new millennium
Atmosphere: A melancholic sense of impending doom, but also . . . gratitude?

This happened to me many years ago in Plant City, Florida. I was going through a rough time as I had broken up with my fiancée, who had cheated on me, and I'd moved in with my sister, her husband, and their three kids. I got a job as a dishwasher at a restaurant and quickly advanced to midday prep and dishwasher. I was making good money, about $13 an hour, which was great for that time. After my breakup, I decided I wanted an entry-level sports car, so I went to a local Mitsubishi dealer and got a 1993 3000GT with low miles.

This was a bit before *The Fast and the Furious*, but I put a couple of thousand dollars into the wheels, speaker system, and engine. I could easily reach 130 miles (209 km) per hour when needed. I made a few friends at work, and we would pile into my 3000GT and go clubbing in the local party district.

One Friday night around 12:30 a.m., we headed to a club called The Machine in the party district. We arrived at the club around 1 a.m., and I had a few Crown and Cokes. After about an hour and a half of unsuccessful attempts to talk to some women, I told

I WAS TERRIFIED WHEN I SAW A DISHEVELED OLD MAN STANDING ON THE INTERSTATE, STARING AT ME.

the guys I was bored and decided to go home. My coworkers had no problem with me leaving. I asked the bartender for a Red Bull and a cup of fountain Coke, quickly downed them, got to my car, and started on my way home.

After a few minutes of driving, I entered the interstate, shifted to fifth gear, and began cruising at around eighty-five miles per hour (137 kph). My sister's house was about an hour's drive from the club, so I usually drove fast to get home before it got too late and disturbed the kids or my sister and her husband.

Looking down at my watch, it read 3:10 a.m. I glanced back up at the interstate, trying to stay focused. There were few cars at this time, which suited me, as I could drive fast without worrying about crashing into another car. I reached my favorite song on the Nine Inch Nails CD that was playing and began drumming on the steering wheel. As I looked out on the interstate, I noticed the light poles becoming more spread out and the woods blurring by on both sides.

For reasons I still can't explain, my CD player skipped, briefly diverting my attention to the car deck and then back up as I drove under an overpass.

I was terrified when I saw a disheveled old man standing on the interstate, staring at me.

Even with my sports car-quality brakes, there was no way I could've stopped before hitting him.

Nevertheless, I locked up my brakes and my tires squealed ear-piercingly loud. Thick white smoke encircled my car. I locked my hands on the steering wheel, shaking. I couldn't take my eyes off the spot where the old man had been, and my breathing was erratic.

Once I managed to stop the car on the side of the highway under an overpass, I got out with my flashlight, its beam cutting through the darkness as I began searching for the old man. I was sure that I had hit and killed him. My mind was racing, my body shaking.

After a few more minutes of searching the area and the overpass itself, something dawned on me. I didn't hear any smashing metal sounds or see any broken glass from my car. Considering the speed at which I was driving, my car would have been wrecked if I had hit somebody.

In my panic, I had forgotten to check my car. I quickly jogged back to the front of it and began surveying it. There was nothing. No blood. No damage. Perfectly fine. It was now 3:33 a.m., according to my watch.

Another odd thing I noticed was that during all this time, no other vehicles had passed by, neither from my side nor the other side of the interstate. I got back into my car, wondering what had just happened. Did I see a road apparition?

Since there was no blood or damage to my car, I decided not to involve the highway troopers to avoid unnecessary questioning about a potential prank call.

It isn't too surprising to see one of these stories take place on Florida's I-4, a stretch of road some consider the most haunted.

According to local folklore, the part of the I-4 near the St. Johns River Bridge is believed to be haunted by the restless spirits of those buried in a forgotten cemetery. Travelers have reported eerie experiences such as drops in temperature, apparitions, and ghostly whispers. Some claim to have seen figures dressed in old-fashioned attire watching the passing cars. The haunting is believed to be a result of the disturbed resting place and tragic history of the immigrant colony nearby. However, not all spirits are unkind, as the narrator in this story may have seen a recently deceased spirit offering a timely warning before moving on.

DID I SEE A ROAD APPARITION?

I shut my door, turned the key, and prepared to get back on the road. As I pulled out from the overpass, my headlights illuminated the apparition again.

It was him! He had this sad, lost look in his eyes. He was wearing a bucket hat, a white polo shirt, brown pants, and black slip-on shoes. He waved at me as if to say, "It's okay, come on. It's safe to go out on the interstate." I was so scared that my foot instinctively pressed on the gas pedal.

However, before I floored it, I quickly gazed out of my driver's side mirror and stomped hard on the brakes. I stopped just when—out of nowhere—a speeding 18-wheeler flew by me, laying on the loud truck horn.

My heart stopped and terror froze me in place. The eighteen-wheeler's red taillights faded quickly over the hill ahead. Gathering my courage, I looked back across the interstate overpass, searching for the old man. There was nothing now. Just an overpass, interstate pole light, and my car. I summoned my courage and got back on the interstate safely, driving home while obeying the speed limit this time.

It was 4:30 a.m. when I pulled into my sister's driveway. It was too late to go inside without waking up the house, so I turned everything off in my car, curled up, and went to sleep right there.

The first thing I saw when I opened my eyes was my sister tapping on my window, urging me to move my car for her husband. Groggily, I did as she asked and walked like a zombie back into the house. She made some coffee and asked why I got back so late. I warned her that she might find it hard to believe what I was about to say. She gave me a skeptical look, so I told her everything.

My sister, a nurse at the local hospital ER, endured six consecutive nights of 12-hour shifts and then enjoyed three days off. As I told her my story, her face grew paler and she drank less of her coffee.

She waited until I finished and then told me something chilling. A week before, on her last night before her three days off, the paramedics brought in an elderly man suffering from Alzheimer's. A car on the interstate had hit him after he wandered from his home that night. The paramedics who found him stated that he had gotten hit under overpass 333 on the interstate—the exact overpass where I had seen the ghost. What's more, my watch had also read 3:33 a.m. at the time I saw him.

She said he was pretty badly injured and died within a few hours. Just before he passed away, however, something odd happened. She went back into his room to check on him, and he was awake. He had the saddest eyes and waved at her, as if beckoning her to come over. But when she got there, his eyes were closed again, and he was unconscious.

At that moment, we both grabbed each other's hands and prayed. Shortly thereafter, I paid off my car, traded it in, and got a Ford F-150. A few weeks later, I met my future wife, and the rest is history, as they say. Looking back, though, if I hadn't looked out my mirror before darting onto the interstate that dark, lonely morning, I wonder if I would've been the next one beckoning sadly to unsuspecting drivers, trying to save them from an unexpected fate.

On October 12, 1979, Roy Fulton, a twenty-six-year-old carpet fitter from Dunstable, UK, gave a lift to a young man on Station Road in the village of Stanbridge. Figuring he was going either to Totternhoe or Dunstable, Fulton came to a halt in front of the hitchhiker who walked along the road toward the van. He wore dark pants, a sweater, and a white-collared shirt. Nothing seemed out of the ordinary. When asked where he wanted to go, his only response was to point ahead, farther down the misty road. Fulton let the man get in the van and they drove on.

The journey continued in silence for some minutes until Fulton decided to offer the youth a cigarette. He leaned forward, picked up the packet of cigarettes, and turned to the man sitting beside him. However, the man was no longer there. Roy Fulton was completely alone.

SMALL TOWNS

Small towns are cozy! Picture a town where everyone knows your name and neighbors are friends. Wouldn't you want to live there?

But they say small towns hide the biggest secrets. Creepy local legends, haunted houses, and fear-inducing forests are common in small towns.

Maybe these towns are small for a reason. Perhaps something chased out much of the population, leaving a terrified few to keep the place running. Who knows, really.

If you're in a rustic mountain town and need to rest, you're welcome to stop by. You should be perfectly fine, so long as you don't go prying for stories and gossip. You might stumble upon something you were never meant to see. Then the once-friendly denizens of that small town may not want you to leave.

These small-town stories are anything but small when it comes to scares.

THE MISSING BOY AND THE PALE MAN

A sudden disappearance of a small boy brings out a search party.
Through the snow and muck, they follow his footsteps. The case and tracks go
cold, but one inhabitant comes close to being the next one to disappear.

FIELD NOTES
Location: A remote, snowy logging town, far from any others
Date/Time: The apex of winter
Atmosphere: The foreboding silence after a snowfall

I'm half Native American and grew up in an isolated town that boasted an impressive
population of ninety-six people in total. In my beliefs, as well as the beliefs of my
community and family, there are benevolent spirits and malevolent spirits. Some are
human, and others are not. Many go unnoticed by people, blending into the background.
Some are retold as stories, legends, and cautionary tales, while others become
notoriously known on the internet, like the Skinwalker and Wendigo.

This is my story about an encounter with a malevolent spirit. I honestly don't know
what I saw and felt, but I know for certain that there was a strange, otherworldly aura
that surrounded a young boy's disappearance within the community, leaving us with
more questions than answers. Whether or not you believe my story, it doesn't change
anything, unfortunately. The boy is still missing and presumed dead and has been for
well over a decade now.

ESP (extrasensory perception) is a highly debated and controversial concept in the field of psychology and paranormal studies. Known as a "sixth sense," it suggests that certain individuals possess the ability to gather information beyond the scope of our five traditional senses. Telepathy refers to the ability to communicate thoughts and feelings directly from one mind to another, regardless of the physical distance between them. Clairvoyance, on the other hand, involves perceiving distant or hidden objects, people, or events that are not accessible through normal sensory channels. Lastly, precognition involves the ability to foresee or predict future events before they occur, seemingly defying the concept of linear time. While scientific research on ESP has produced mixed results, many people continue to report personal experiences that they attribute to these extraordinary phenomena.

Calling where I lived a "rural town" is putting it politely. We were extremely remote; the nearest town was well over an hour away. In my town, most of its inhabitants belonged to the same tribe. It was a small logging town tucked deep into the mountains. Everyone knew each other and everyone knew the same local superstitions and stories.

There were quite a few unusual stories surrounding the forest in our town, some of them involving inhuman spirits. I had explored those forests since I was very small, probably too small. I have vivid memories of being alone in the deep forest at three or four years old, feeling completely safe as if there was a protective presence. I'd return time and time again to feel safe, where the weight of my neglectful and abusive family lifted from my shoulders.

There were other things in the forest that I can't really describe, but when you lived there, you learned over time how to "read" the forest, whether it was safe to be in or if you needed to keep your wits about you. Occasionally, you could feel something in the dark edges waiting there, as if needing an invitation to come closer.

Sometimes, that dark presence would follow. Many times, when I was older and riding my bike along the old logging trails, I felt it. There was always this familiar but unsettling feeling. Sometimes, you could hear it call your name—but I never answered when it did. A nagging instinct inside me warned against acknowledging it, speaking to it, or inviting it any closer.

And then, as soon as it had appeared, it was gone, and the serenity from the forest would return. This was kind of the usual thing for most of us living out there, especially the loggers. It was just one of those things that we knew was unnatural, but something we lived with—keeping it on the outskirts—until someone invited it in.

The boy who went missing.

I can't be sure what happened. I can only provide insights into this case based on my own encounters, as well as the accounts and observations of others.

On a winter's day, with nearly two feet (61 cm) of snowfall overnight, this boy vanished. He uncharacteristically left his home that morning and simply disappeared. It caused immediate panic; a local search and rescue party had mobilized before law enforcement could reach us.

The boy suffered from health problems and required medication to function correctly—medication that he, again uncharacteristically, did not take with him. The last witness provided directions as to his whereabouts, and his footprints were promptly discovered in the snow.

This is where things become strange. Law enforcement arrived, accompanied by additional search and rescue operatives. They brought along search and rescue canines, ready to sniff out any signs of the missing person. Additionally, they came with durable terrain gear, such as snowmobiles and climbing equipment that were ready to conquer the challenging landscape.

Law enforcement followed the boy's footprints off-road and through terrain that they had extreme difficulty navigating through, even with all their gear. In some cases, it was impossible to get through. Yet, the boy's footprints persisted on for miles, until search and rescue operatives noted something disturbing.

At some point, seemingly out of nowhere, the boy's footprints were joined by the footprints of someone, or something else. They were described as long strides that looked as if they were leading the boy deeper in, and then both sets of footprints vanished for miles in the snow, like something pulled them into the sky without a trace.

Several miles away, a secondary team that had gone ahead in the boy's direction of travel radioed that they had found his footprints again and could validate them as his by the unique design on the soles of his shoes. Again, the same thing happened. The footprints started as his alone, but they were later joined by "something" else before vanishing once more. The search began in the morning and went on well into the night.

It wasn't until the next day that one of the boy's shoes and his hoodie washed up where the river emptied. They never found his body. Shortly after, he was presumed to have succumbed to the elements, but the search efforts persisted for an extended period.

Earlier in my story, I mentioned locals could "feel" the forest and things present in it, including that dark presence that lingered just out of reach, following, speaking our names. After the boy disappeared, this thing was no longer on the outskirts. Its presence seemed to fuse with the forest itself.

I mentioned that when I was younger, I would go into the forest to feel safe and secure. Shortly after the boy went missing, I went to visit my secret place in the woods like I had thousands of times before, but suddenly I couldn't.

What I mean is that I got to the edge of our property, and I could not force my body to pass through our gate and into the forest. My body froze and trembled as my heartbeat thudded loudly in my ears, and my legs turned to jelly.

This suffocating sense of doom felt like it was crushing the life out of me.

To put it in layman's terms, I felt like if I were to go into that forest at that time, I was going to die—that I would also be "taken." Those words were being forced into my brain from something I couldn't see but felt familiar and nauseating.

My instincts immediately recognized that familiar entity from my childhood, asserting its presence and needing no one's permission. It made the forest change from feeling peaceful and alive to sick and decaying, a stagnant place where no light could reach anymore.

AT SOME POINT, SEEMINGLY OUT OF NOWHERE, THE BOY'S FOOTPRINTS WERE JOINED BY THE FOOTPRINTS OF SOMEONE, OR SOMETHING ELSE.

(I tried to go back several other times, and I had the same reaction each time. Even my ex-husband, when I took him there, had a similar reaction despite my not giving him any backstory about the place. He was a firefighter who specialized in wildland and forest fires, and even he stopped at the gate and silently stared into the trees. I could see goosebumps rising on the back of his neck. He even said that he didn't know what it was, but it felt like he was going to die if he went there.)

Strange things kept happening after the boy went missing. Previously secure sections of the mountain road became plagued with one accident after another, as drivers claimed to have encountered mysterious figures obstructing their path or experienced sudden loss of control over their vehicles.

People drink a lot in this area. The sad truth is that a lot of these same people drive themselves home after drinking, so many of the townspeople kind of shrugged off the increase in car accidents and attributed them to the local café finally getting their liquor license. I thought this was closer to the truth myself until it happened to me.

I was driving home from work. It was dark. Rounding a corner, I spotted what I initially mistook for a tall, thin, pale, and maybe unclothed individual standing near the road sign. I immediately glanced in the side view mirror of my car as I slowed down to get a better look, to see if this person was hurt or needed help—as it was below freezing—and they looked very nude at first glance. But then I felt that familiar suffocating feeling of dread and nausea.

What I saw . . . I sometimes still can't accept. It was definitely humanoid, but there was something off about it; the more I looked at it, the more my instincts screamed it was not a human being.

WHERE ITS EYES SHOULD HAVE BEEN WAS EMPTY, BUT STILL REFLECTING THE LIGHT FROM MY CAR, LIKE WHEN YOU SHINE A LIGHT ON A CAT'S OR DOG'S EYES IN THE DARK.

The skin appeared ghostly pale, with a texture reminiscent of well-worn leather.

Both the arms and legs were excessively long, as were the fingers.

The hands and feet of this thing were black, like they had been caked in ash and coal from the fireplace.

It had no hair.

It had no ears, except what might have been holes where the ears once were.

Where its eyes should have been was empty, but still reflecting the light from my car, like when you shine a light on a cat's or dog's eyes in the dark.

There was no nose and no lips.

What I hoped was mud, or charcoal, covered its gaping mouth.

I didn't know what I was looking at, but I knew it wasn't human—and I got the hell out of there as fast as I could. It wasn't until I returned home and began sketching what I witnessed that I grasped the true height of this entity—a minimum of seven to eight feet (2 m), surpassing even our towering road signs designed for snowy conditions.

When I searched for what I saw, most of the results pointed toward the "Rake," a ghostly cryptid that I had never heard of before. The images I found of it were eerily reminiscent of the thing I encountered.

Similarly, those features can also fit a true Wendigo, that in Algonquin lore do not look like gangly men wearing a deer skull for a head as they are often portrayed, but the geographical location isn't right, even though I am from one of the Algonquin tribes from where that lore originated.

I've since moved out of my childhood hometown, but this entire event is something that has stayed with me in the back of my mind since then. I don't know what happened to the boy, and I don't know what that thing was that I saw—but it definitely left an impact on me and those who encountered it. The forest, once a place of solace and comfort, became a place of darkness and fear.

The Mannegishi, originating from the Native American Cree Nation, are believed to be mischievous beings with a penchant for trickery. Standing at about three feet (1 m) tall, they possess a lanky frame with long arms and an unusual six fingers on each hand. However, their most distinctive characteristic is their lack of a nose, which is replaced by a smooth, featureless face. Their heads are disproportionately large, adding to their peculiar appearance. They also bear the pale skin that is common with these humanoid cryptids.

According to Cree legends, these creatures were created by the Great Spirit as a test of human gullibility and trustworthiness. They are known for their ability to shapeshift and deceive unsuspecting individuals. In modern times, the existence of these beings is often linked to the Dover Demon, a mysterious creature first sighted in 1977 in Dover, Massachusetts. The Dover Demon's description shares similarities with the Mannegishi, suggesting a possible connection between the two species. However, the true nature and intentions of these beings remain shrouded in mystery, making them a subject of fascination and intrigue.

SHIRLEY, WISCONSIN

A group of friends search for a fabled haunted cemetery. But while they set up base in a nearby town, they discover it is the town itself that is haunted.

FIELD NOTES

Location: Outside a rumored haunted cemetery in Shirley, Wisconsin, USA
Date/Time: A time suitable for ghost hunting, in 2008
Atmosphere: An ethereal, hazy sense of something feeling horribly out of place

In 2008, I was eighteen years old. At the time, a couple of friends of mine decided we were going to start ghost hunting. We wanted to go somewhere away from the small Wisconsin town we all grew up in. I live about thirty minutes away from Green Bay, Wisconsin, and one of my friends was looking for haunted locations around this area—somewhere far enough to make it special, but not too far.

We decided on a small town called Shirley. There was a reported haunted cemetery there where you could see a light floating in the cemetery's corner and hear voices and crying—typical haunted cemetery stuff. We had a good ol' fashioned VHS camcorder that we recorded with. It had an old-school light on it. It got the job done for a group of eighteen-to-twenty-year-olds who, on a whim, went ghost hunting.

My friend Cece and I were very excited about this trip. We stayed up late at night engrossed in conversation and laughter, creating amusing "what if" scenarios that left us in stitches. Two other friends, Momo and her boyfriend Lewis, were joining us on this trip.

On the day of, we set out as planned in Lewis's car. Cece was sitting in the back seat with me, while Momo was in the passenger's seat and Lewis was driving. I was sitting

behind Lewis, and Cece sat behind Momo. We headed toward Green Bay; Shirley was about fifteen to twenty minutes past it.

It was nighttime, and the stars were out. We were all excited: in a good mood, smoking cigarettes, making jokes. Cece and I couldn't stop laughing at each other in the back seat. She and I had developed an inside joke by saying, "Ya know what's messed up?" which was our way of saying, "I was just thinking the same thing." Depending on our tone, the statement came out as serious or humorous.

It got to a point where we kept saying it so much that we were saying things in unison. We both noticed how strange this was, and we did our best to avoid it, so we tried engaging in conversation with Momo and Lewis.

But then, Cece and I started joking about a hypothetical situation in the cemetery where she would hold a rubber chicken in her hand for a laugh, and in the same rhythm, in the same way, she and I both made a ridiculous gobbling noise. It was eerily in sync, and it kept happening. We stopped talking for a while because it was freaking Cece out.

During the car ride, everyone noticed shooting stars—a lot of shooting stars. However, I didn't see any. Every five minutes, one of the other three would say they saw one. I started thinking they were just messing with me.

When I looked out the window, I saw many stars, but they were all still. I grew frustrated and said in a jokingly angry tone, "Just show me one shoo—"

Before I could even finish my angry plea, a star shot across my line of vision. I was in awe. It was impossible. I couldn't even believe it. The timing was perfect, as if the cosmos were saying, "Shut up."

I also couldn't help but notice that on the way to Shirley, we had no cars behind us. We were on the highway in Green Bay, a popular city, but no cars passed us, and we didn't pass any cars. We also didn't see any headlights behind us, except for some taillights in front. There was never any close traffic.

Now, I couldn't tell you about any of the signage leading up to Shirley, but getting on the road to this town was almost surreal. It was like parts of the road didn't make sense. There were trees and road signs in strange places. I remember driving through a very small town that had a gas station and not

Shirley is "surely" a small town. While nothing of note typically happens in that small town, possibly named after a brand of paint, the graveyard in the story exists and is just as hard to find as depicted. An individual posted on a Proboards forum looking for more simple instructions. These were the directions given:

"Green Bay – Shirley – West Shirley Rd. – Going West on Shirley Rd. in the Town of Shirley, there is a stone-covered road where a very old cemetery is. This cemetery glows of [sic] a pale green light, at times from an area of headstones in the South-East Corner. And it is reported to have followed people."

Could our intrepid ghost hunters have somehow momentarily pierced the veil between the living and dead, turning Shirley into a metaphorical ghost town?

much else: a couple of streetlights and a veterinarian, or a chiropractor, or a dentist? I don't remember.

All I knew was that we had to turn left to get onto the road that led to Shirley. And this wasn't even the main road to the town. The main road to Shirley was a long, straight road with notable hills. It was strange that there were no cars in sight, neither behind us, nor in front of us, nor coming from the opposite direction. It was surreal. At one point, there was a deer standing on the side of the road, watching us drive by. Then another one. And another one. All males. It was strange.

The center of Shirley included a mill, two bars, and old buildings that may have been turned into apartments. It looked like there were lights on in the windows, but it was hard to tell. We drove down the road where the cemetery was located and passed by a church that had another cemetery next to it, but it wasn't the one we were looking for.

Shirley's roads were quite empty, with only a few farmhouses and barns in sight. Of the houses we saw, it was as if each one had five to six lights outside—not including decorations or solar lights, but actual bright lights on the house: garage, barn, and even poles in the fields were all lit up. Lights just kept appearing,

THEN WE SAW THE CAR TAKE A LEFT TURN, BUT WE NEVER CAME ACROSS THAT CURVE IN THE ROAD.

although some of them disappeared as we got closer. Throughout the whole time, there were still no cars around us and there was no movement in the town.

We parked outside the cemetery next to the church and tried to film something from the car. None of us felt like getting out, mostly because we all couldn't help but notice that it didn't feel normal outside. We stuck our hands and heads outside, and it just felt wrong. Like if we got out of the car, we couldn't get back in. So, none of us wanted to even attempt to get out.

There was a field to the right with tall corn that was ready, if not beyond ready, to get cut down.

Momo took the camera and passed it to Lewis, who filmed the cemetery. Then he passed the camera back to Momo. This happened a couple of times. Out of nowhere, we noticed a car driving away from us.

Lewis decided he was going to follow it, though he had no reason to. He wanted to catch up to it, but he couldn't. He kept increasing his speed, but the car ahead of us maintained its distance. It's possible they thought we were up to no good or wanted to harm them. But no matter how hard we tried, we couldn't get close to this car. It seemed like it didn't have a backplate, which is illegal. Then we saw the car take a left turn, but we never came across that curve in the road. We all questioned if it had actually turned there, as there were no roads to the left, just fields. It was inexplicable.

Eventually, we saw a truck driving toward us. It was dark and we couldn't see who was driving it, but it became a pattern. Every time we saw headlights approaching, it was a truck.

The same truck.

It had no front license plate and kept driving by us as if it had multiple streets to turn down and surprise us with. We also noticed three vehicles coming toward us, and to our surprise, they were all similar trucks, appearing at perfect intervals.

None of them had license plates. All the taillights disappeared behind us. And despite that, there was never a car behind us.

The initial excitement faded. None of us wanted to get out of the car because of the fear of falling into the false reality of Shirley. After attempting to follow another car that disappeared on the same road as the previous one, we decided it was time to go. However, I insisted on going back to the cemetery, saying I would get out of the car if we did. Strangely, headlights suddenly materialized behind us, radiating a sinister and hostile aura. They didn't seem like a car casually popping up, but more like an evil pair of headlights.

It freaked Lewis out and he said we were leaving. He turned onto the road we had taken to enter Shirley, driving well above the speed limit—but the headlights were still behind us, keeping up with our speed.

He drove faster, and they followed suit. We were going over eighty-five miles per hour (137 kph); the lights behind us started disappearing behind the hills of the road, never to reappear. Stranger still, all the lights we had seen on the way in were turned off, and not a single bulb stayed lit.

When we reached the road to leave Shirley, we felt relieved. There was an old car about to turn into Shirley, but they waited for us to turn onto the road they were on, even though no cars were coming. We watched them for a while; they had plenty of time to turn. As our headlights hit the side of the car, I looked inside to see who was going to Shirley, but I saw nothing except for a black silhouette.

I asked if anyone else saw the driver. They all said no. Either they didn't notice or didn't care to look. But I did. How could headlights obscure someone's features? I should have seen their face; I tested this theory many times. Also, note that this was the first sedan we encountered, not a truck like the others.

I felt relieved to be on that road. I was filled with confusion, frustration, and unanswered questions. What was going on in Shirley? Thoughts plagued my mind; everyone else remained silent, as if drained. I was looking at my phone or something else, although phones weren't very entertaining yet.

It's no surprise that cemeteries would be a hotbed for paranormal activity. But which one of the thousands out there in the world is the most haunted?

St. Louis Cemetery No. 1, in the heart of New Orleans, holds a long and dark history that contributes to its reputation as the most haunted cemetery in the world. Established in 1789, this cemetery is not only the ultimate resting place for many influential figures, but is also a hub for supernatural activity. Local legends and ghost stories have perpetuated the belief that the spirits of the deceased still wander among the tombs.

One of the most famous apparitions is the ghost of Voodoo Queen Marie Laveau, who is said to appear to those seeking her mystical powers. As visitors walk through the cemetery's labyrinthine paths, they may encounter chilling occurrences such as hearing disembodied screams or witnessing ethereal figures lurking in the shadows. The eerie atmosphere is further intensified by the presence of ghostly animals, with cats and dogs being frequently spotted roaming the grounds. Brave individuals who dare to record the cemetery's mystique in photographs have reported capturing strange orbs or ghostly apparitions, solidifying the belief in the otherworldly presence that permeates St. Louis Cemetery No. 1.

I remember I was texting a friend when, out of the corner of my eye, I noticed Cece slowly turning her head to look out the back window. Suddenly, she started crying hysterically, catching me off guard.

I asked her, "What's wrong?" and looked out the back window of the car.

As we looked back, we saw a dead-end road with an old ball-top streetlamp, its light flickering weakly amid the surrounding trees. The dead end we had just come from. And under that light stood a being in a white cloak and gown, resembling a white grim reaper. I couldn't see their face as the hood covered it, but I could feel them looking at me. It felt like I stared at them for minutes, although it was only seconds. Then I remembered why I looked behind us.

I turned to my crying friend, put my hand on her shoulder, and asked, "What did you see? Tell me what you saw!"

Between sobs, she choked out, "I saw a man dressed in white standing by the side of the road. He tried to open your door. I saw him out of the corner of my eye through Lewis's window." Her words were shaky and hysterical, and I strained to understand them. "When I looked up, he was reaching for your door. Then I followed him with my eyes, and the road changed. Then I looked away."

I couldn't believe it, but I told her I saw the same thing.

She couldn't comprehend what she was seeing, and neither could I. It was as if we were the only two in the car. Lewis and Momo remained silent, asking nothing, not even looking behind the car. It seemed like they didn't want to. It was almost as if something was telling us to stay out.

Momo and Lewis later explained that they didn't say anything because they felt like they didn't care. Their emotions were absent. They didn't look behind them or use their mirrors to check what was happening behind us. They just stared ahead, as if everything had turned black and white.

We went back to Shirley a couple of times, but nothing compared to the first visit. I don't know what made it so special; maybe it was the day, the energy, or our desire for something paranormal.

We went to Shirley in search of a cemetery we never found, but we left with a truly disturbing story to tell. Some people don't believe us, but it doesn't matter. We know what happened. I can't help but wonder if anyone else ever experienced it and if they got out of the car or got chased like we did. Either way, when we returned to my apartment, we watched the bit of video we had recorded.

We saw the trucks, the taillights, the random lights in the town, and even a few moments where the lens flare from three barn lights resembled the white hooded figure that watched us from the side. This made Cece cry hysterically again. The only evidence we have of the spooky side of Shirley is when Lewis gave Momo the camera while we were parked by the cornfield during our adventure.

In the video, a man with a straw hat and overalls emerges from the cornfield, his gaze fixed on us, yet he appears to be floating without legs.

HIDING FROM A HIGHLAND MONSTER

The stillness offered by nature's isolation offers both peace and terror.
A monster guided only by sound hunts its prey, guided only by fear.

FIELD NOTES

Location: The Scottish Highlands, UK
Date/Time: A summer's day, hot enough to take a dip in the local lake
Atmosphere: A desperate urgency to run away

I live in Scotland, UK. I won't say exactly where, but it's pretty rural. I've lived here my whole life and never spent more than my university years away.

I'd never had any spooky supernatural experiences or creepy ghost stories. I wasn't a believer in any of that. I'm no stranger to the woods or the glens. I find enjoyment in camping, hiking, and swimming in nature. Even when I'm at home, I like to chill out on the porch while on my phone.

I always felt so comfortable surrounded by nature. I suppose it helps to know that the UK has no dangerous animals, and the fact I live a good jaunt away from even the smallest town—so no people to worry about either. Where I live provides complete seclusion, just the way I like it.

But I finally had my first spooky encounter and honestly, I'm not really sure what happened. I've told a few close friends, one of whom encouraged me to tell my story. She said it'll help me come to terms with it. I hope she's right.

Despite the stereotypes about the Scottish Highlands, we do get summer here, and it can get boiling and sunny on the right day. It was that sort of day when I figured I'd go to the small lake about forty minutes from my house and take a dip.

The journey there followed the same pattern as always: woods, field, hill, more woods, and finally a clearing with the lake. It's my little slice of heaven. It's so beautiful. The water trickles down from higher up, so it's crystal clear. Honestly, it looks like something out of a fancy commercial.

I threw off my clothes just down to my swimming suit and jumped in. The lake's about the width of an average canal, for reference, and deep enough that I can only just touch the bottom on my tiptoes. Granted, I'm not the tallest lass.

I swam for a while and just enjoyed cooling off. For the record, it was about 11:30 a.m., and that was when the first weird thing happened. A loud ruckus in the bushes made me jump as, suddenly, three deer came tearing through, jumped over a shallower part of the water, and off into the other side of the woods, the way I'd come up from.

Now, this was really strange. I'm not quiet when I swim. I splash around and typically sing to myself when I'm in the mood, which I was. The deer around here aren't used to humans, so they avoid coming anywhere near you. Throughout my entire life, I had only seen a few from a distance. So, for them to run toward my noisy self without glancing at me was off. In hindsight, I know now why they were running so blindly, but we'll get to that.

I was a little uneasy. I knew that rationally they were probably just in season or something, but it just didn't sit right with me. After a few more minutes, I got out of the water and decided I'd walk back home. Usually, I towel off by the river, get re-dressed, and then head off, but this time, I just didn't want to hang around there any longer than I already had.

I threw on my shirt and trousers as quickly as I could and made a move back down the way I'd come, where the deer had gone. Yes, I was still soaking wet. I had just figured the warm weather would dry me off, but I had made one stupid mistake. Thanks to not wanting to faff around with the laces, I had left my boots in my bag and opted to walk home barefoot.

The monster in this story has short and stark white fur, giving it a fearsome appearance. Disregarding its fur, though, the features bear a striking resemblance to the cryptids known as Pale Crawlers. According to folklore, Pale Crawlers are elusive creatures that inhabit remote, desolate areas. This creature is possibly the inspiration behind the popular internet-based horror story known as "The Rake" (see page 186).

Pale Crawlers are described as having long limbs and a hunched posture, sporting sickly pale skin. Did the potential Crawler in this story suffer grave injuries or sickness, causing its beaten state and making it more aggressive?

Heading back, the woods seemed strange. Birds were very vocal, bugs were buzzing like mad, and I kept catching glimpses of wild rabbits. Just like the deer, everything was quickly moving away downward, downwind.

I grew more and more alarmed, which is very out of character for me. My pace quickened to just shy of a jog. I looked around frantically, as if I was trying to spot something, though I had no idea what. I can't say I had some feeling of being watched or stalked, but it was more like I felt unwelcome: in the wrong place, that kind of thing.

Thanks to the animals going nuts, mainly the birds up in the branches, I couldn't hear much of anything else. That's why it took me so off guard. For nearly ten minutes, I looked around until I noticed something different as I shifted my gaze to the right. I saw a figure clearly; it was keeping pace with me, shadowing me, and staring straight at me.

I'm still not 100 percent sure what it looked like. It had a slender figure, body covered in a thin layer of stark-white hair and moving with a smooth yet loping gait. I know it turned its head to face me, but, as strange as it sounds, I have no clue what its face looked like. It's like I saw it and my gaze just slipped off it, like I instinctively averted my gaze to the trees and bushes.

My heart skipped a beat. I almost tripped over myself in sheer shock. I can't quite remember my thought process, but it was something like, "What is that and how long

I CAN'T SAY I HAD SOME FEELING OF BEING WATCHED OR STALKED, BUT IT WAS MORE LIKE I FELT UNWELCOME: IN THE WRONG PLACE, THAT KIND OF THING.

has it been keeping up with me? What does it want? What should I do?" all at once. Some trees came between me and the thing I'd glimpsed, and I just stopped dead.

My entire being resonated with an intense alarm, signaling imminent danger, yet advising against fleeing. I don't know why, but my immediate thought was to climb the nearest tree and take it from there.

In equal measure, I both wanted to see it again—to figure out what the hell it was—but also to never set eyes on it again. It shook my whole body to the core. I felt sick and dizzy trying to wrap my head around it. As strange as it sounds, when I'd seen it for that split second, I felt offended. I felt genuinely disgusted deep down, knowing that this thing existed so close that I could see the bushes being pushed down as it clambered through them.

My messed-up state aside, I made it up the tree and tried to catch my breath on a decently large branch. I had to sit on the larger part and balance myself by using my feet to press against the other part of the trunk. It was one of those trees that grow into a kind of Y shape.

For a few moments, I sat there, slowly scanning the forest floor below. It was dead silent. All the freaked-out animals had booked it far away. It was just me, my tree, my pounding heart, and the consuming fear that *it* was still around. I wasn't sure if I missed its approach because of the birds or if it was simply silent. The idea only made me feel even more queasy.

After what felt like ages, I spotted the slightest rustle in a patch of bushes. I heard it breathing, or maybe sniffing. It was doglike, but silent. It almost seemed to come from all around me. Then the bushes rustled again, and it stopped.

While stuck up that damned tree, I was petrified, staying as still as I could and desperately listening out for anything at all.

Now, this is where my haste in leaving the river came back to mess with me. I felt something on my right foot. There was something small, almost imperceptible, at first glance. However, there was another, and then another, and even more. Like tiny touches, super light but moving. I tilted my head to see, only to realize the cause. It was ants. Tiny black specks pouring out of little holes in the bark and toward my feet.

Fortunately, the ants in the UK are not usually the biting type. I almost wish they had been, in retrospect. It would've been easier to ignore. No, these little guys did something far worse. They tickled. At first, they were just barely noticeable, but as more and more climbed onto my feet, it quickly became unbearable. You'd think when you're scared to death, you'd be able to ignore something so silly. Hell, normally I'm not even a ticklish person—but it heightened my senses to the max, paranoid about this thing that was still down in the woods somewhere.

Just as I was going to pull my feet away and move how I was sitting, I saw it again. It just strolled out brazenly into the open. Its head was held high, sniffing the air. My eyes tried to move off it from sheer reflex, but this time I forced myself to look at it.

Despite being hunched over, it still stood taller than anyone I had ever met. Long, bony arms rested on the ground like a gorilla, a visible spine pushing against the patchy white fur. Its face, though: I'd never seen anything like it. I can't even think of an animal to compare it to. I guess the best I could say would be like an incredibly malnourished cow. It had no horns and large, pointy ears like a canine, but its disfigured face was a sight to behold.

That's when I noticed several things all at once. Its mouth was slightly open, drooling and lined with mismatched, jagged teeth. Its nostrils were bloodied, with one completely collapsed. Finally, it was looking straight at me. Here's the thing, though— it was blind. It had these sickly, pus-filled, milky eyes. It was looking straight at me, sniffing, but had no idea I was a few meters away. I could've spat and probably hit it.

I tried to stay as still as humanly possible, staring at this abomination. The ants, however, had different plans. When I say they were covering my feet, I mean it. I was having to balance myself by pressing just my toes against the bark. Like I said earlier, I'm not a tall girl, and this meant they were all over the undersides of my poor feet.

I couldn't even move a hand to cover my mouth with how I was balancing. It was insane. I was staring down at this completely unnatural thing, and all I could do was try not to giggle. I tried to move one foot away, but the second I so much as knocked a leafy branch, the creature's ears twitched and its head snapped to where the sound came from. Putting my foot back, however, only seemed to shake the bark and cause even more ants to come exploring.

The creature was coming closer, meandering toward the tree, sniffing so loudly it was almost wheezing. It reached the bottom of the tree and lifted its head. Then came its first arm. It was so long it almost reached where I was immediately. I saw its hand, a gnarled mess of curved claws jutting out of knuckles, almost like that of a sloth. Its claws sunk into the bark like it was nothing. Then, it reared up and, from what I can tell, prepared to climb.

I was weighing up my options. Should I jump out of the tree and make a run for it? But I knew I couldn't outrun this thing—and if I jumped out of the tree from this height, I would probably break my ankle and be in real trouble. Staying still was my other option, hoping it would pass by without noticing, but I knew it would probably catch my scent from being so close. Then, ever-present, were my little tormentors.

Just as I thought I was going to either pass out or let a few giggles slip past my trembling lips, something like a miracle happened. In the distance, a sound rang out. It was quiet, but in such silence, it could still be heard. It was a car door slamming shut.

The creature's whole body twisted, then it tore off into the woods at a terrifying speed. It even ripped a fist-sized hole in the tree where its claws had been. The moment I had the opportunity, I swiftly withdrew my feet from the ants and held my hand over my mouth, releasing a combination of laughter and tears that had been suppressed for a long time. I climbed down the tree with less care than I should have, cutting my palm on some of the broken bark on my way down.

Once I was on solid ground, I shook the remaining ants off and made a beeline for home. I desperately wanted to run, but I knew I couldn't risk making a sound. Though jumpy and paranoid, I closed the distance and got out of the woods and

Scotland is host to many interesting and unique stories of cryptids and folklore. The Bean-nighe, as the legend goes, frequently appears wearing a tattered gray cloak and has wild and unkempt hair. She is said to have pale, ghostly skin and piercing, otherworldly eyes. When she appears as a hag, she emanates an eerie aura that sends chills down the spines of those who encounter her. However, she possesses the ability to transform into a stunningly beautiful woman, captivating anyone who sees her with her ethereal beauty. Despite her haunting presence, the Bean-nighe is not inherently malevolent. She prepares departed souls for their journey to the afterlife. If approached by a living person, the outcome can vary. Some may receive a foreboding warning or a glimpse into the future if they approach her, while others may be granted a blessing or even a small act of kindness. However, it is believed that engaging with the Bean-nighe comes with a certain risk, as one may be tempted to meddle with fate or be overwhelmed by her supernatural presence.

into my house. I was even careful to shut the door quietly. After all, that slamming car door sounded like it was ages away, and my house was only about ten minutes from where I'd just hidden.

I haven't seen it since, though I've hardly been outside since that incident. The few close friends I've told all believe me. Thankfully, they know I'm not the sort to joke about and prank people. I'm unsure what occurred with the car and the unfortunate individual entering or exiting. I hope they're okay. I'm worried about cutting my hand on the bark, I have to admit. What if that thing gets my scent from it? Maybe I'm just still too shaken from it all.

Well, that's my story. I think writing it out has helped a little, even if reliving it has left me feeling quite jittery. Stay safe, everyone—and well, I know it sounds cliché, but I really mean it. Be careful in the woods. It doesn't matter what's "supposed" to live there. Nature doesn't play by our rules, and there are things we don't know still out there. This has cemented it for me: there really is no such thing as a "safe" forest.

WICKED WOODS

Forests remain unclaimed by humans; their thick green canopies act as shrouds of defiance. Thorns, apex predators, and poisonous fungi guard Mother Nature's domain.

But who's to say nature doesn't weave together monstrous things from our nightmares to keep us away? Skinwalker, wendigo, werewolf: creatures born from primal fears. Despite being considered legends, never having existed or disappeared long ago, there are contemporary eyewitness accounts of creatures matching their descriptions.

So maybe they have always existed. Where would the legends have originated, if not from ancient encounters? Stories passed down as warnings, giving rise to infamous legends. Before it was a nighttime story to keep children afraid of climbing out of bed, the Bogeyman started somewhere. Sadly, our world is filled with bogeymen, many of whom lurk in the woods, waiting for unsuspecting hikers or hunters. Survivors have stories to tell, including the ones about terrible things in the woods that you'll soon see in this section.

Encounters that may themselves end up as bedtime stories for our descendants.

THE WHISTLER

Our desire for safety will have us searching for rational explanations. Surely that was just your voice echoing off the trees? Surely it can't be anything else?

FIELD NOTES

Location: Farmland in an undisclosed location, USA
Date/Time: Evening twilight, in early November
Atmosphere: The unsettled feeling of someone hanging onto your every word

I was a freshly graduated high school student on my way to college when I had this encounter. During my senior year, I had a job working for my grandfather on his two farms as a farmhand—or more accurately, a farm manager. He would give me instructions on what to do at the farm when he wasn't there, most commonly feeding the cows.

It was early November, and baseball practice started after school. It would last from 3:25 to 5:30 p.m., and by the time I arrived at work, the sun was almost down. I started getting ready after arriving. One day, I had dressed up, filled the buckets, and fed the animals on the first farm when I realized I didn't have a key to the second. Frustrated, it forced me to pick up two buckets at a time and walk them from the fence to the feed troughs, which was a good forty-yard (37 m) walk.

While walking, I tried to keep myself upbeat and started whistling. It wasn't a real pattern or tune, just something I came up with. When I returned and put the last buckets in the truck bed, I heard something from the neighboring property; it was a whistle. The absence of anyone living nearby made it strange. It sounded very close, but I rationalized it as a mockingbird or something and went on with my life.

Despite my self-imposed ban on whistling, the strange melodic sound of whistling continued to echo around me for the next couple of days. Slowly, over those few days, it got clearer and clearer until it sounded like regular whistling, eventually growing louder. Initially, it was very faint, almost drowned out by the sound of my footsteps. It was more like the rushing of wind. But in those few days, I had become accustomed to the whistling and even expected it.

Then, one day, it didn't come, and I felt a little disappointed. This time, I had brought the key, and as I walked up to the gate and started fiddling with my keys, I dropped them into the grass.

"Dammit!" I spoke.

As I squatted to search for the keys, I heard a very faint sound coming from the other property, a low groan or gurgle. It started growing louder. At this point, I felt more curious than scared about what was happening over there.

I left my truck parked across from the property and walked a few feet down the road. Then, I hopped the fence and entered the property where I heard the sounds.

There are several cryptids that are said to mimic the voices of humans. Skinwalkers are the most common, but there are others lurking in the weeds, like the sinister Fleshgait.

Fleshgaits are mysterious creatures that are often described as tall, slender, and with glowing eyes that can change color. They have smooth and graceful movements, allowing them to navigate through various environments effortlessly. Witnesses have reported encounters in both remote wooded areas and suburban neighborhoods. Their unique ability to mimic voices and appearances sets them apart, allowing them to lure unsuspecting prey. Theories suggest that Fleshgaits possess advanced anatomical knowledge because of the lack of evidence of internal organs or struggle after an attack.

The property had a steep uphill terrain and was covered with thick vegetation. The farther up I went, the denser the vegetation became.

I should have paid attention to how the gurgling remained just as faint as before even as I headed up the hill. Along the way, a foul smell hit my nose—a strange mixture of garbage and wet dog.

As I was about to crest the hill, I heard it clearly: a drawn-out and almost sinister replication of my curse from earlier. The voice stretched each letter in the words until snapping into the next. My "dammit" echoed back in a cruel and low groan.

It sounded as if a sixty-year-old smoker said "dammit" slowly. I automatically thought someone was on our property. Feeling somewhat angry and paranoid, I started moving slower, not wanting this person to hear me before I could see them. I continued cautiously, stopping and listening when I heard the word again. This time it wasn't as drawn out and eerie. It felt more like just a normal person seeing how slowly they could say it.

I sat on a log, trying to figure out what I should do about this person who kept repeating "dammit." I noticed that their tone was getting higher, and their inflection was changing. It suddenly hit me that whoever this was, they were trying

IT SUDDENLY HIT ME THAT WHOEVER THIS WAS, THEY WERE TRYING TO PERFECTLY MIMIC ME, SLOWLY HONING IN ON MY TONE, INFLECTION, AND EVEN MY FRUSTRATION WHEN I SAID IT.

to perfectly mimic me, slowly honing in on my tone, inflection, and even my frustration when I said it. Feeling angry and somewhat scared now, I got up and continued to crest the hill. I flicked on the flashlight on my phone and shouted, "Hey! This is private property!" However, I was cut off mid-sentence.

As I came over the hill, the light barely illuminated a naked figure squatting just a couple of yards in front of me. The glow of my flashlight faintly illuminated the figure's eyes, and I immediately sensed that something was wrong. This wasn't a regular person. Their unusually long neck stretched out, and as I approached, they jerked their neck and swiftly turned their head to lock eyes with me, their body remaining completely still. Their eyes were too large, and their head was large and slender.

They remained squatted in a ballerina-like pose. I glanced at their body. They were extremely skinny, and their ribs were visible through their skin. There was a brief silence, and then, like a robot, the figure turned and slowly stood with their hands at their side. I questioned whether this was even a person.

They were far too tall to be a person.

"Dammit," it said in my voice, the words no longer drawn out.

Without looking back, I sprinted down the hill. It didn't feel like running; it felt like my legs were simply going through the motions. I didn't dare glance back before reaching the fence. As soon as I hopped it, I got in my truck and sped away.

Unfortunately, I still work at that farm, but I've never told anyone this story, not even my grandfather. I've only heard the whistling a few more times since then.

VISIT IN THE WOODS

Fooled into thinking he knows all the forest can throw at him, a hunter steadies his rifle. He is unaware that beyond the safety of his scope is a threat from beyond.

FIELD NOTES

Location: In the thick of the woods, anywhere
Date/Time: A windy day during hunting season
Atmosphere: The quiet serenity of being all alone in the woods

The woods can be a scary place, but I still love being out there, even after this encounter that I'm about to tell you.

Allow me to establish the layout of the land and the design of my blind, a small structure carefully crafted to conceal a hunter from wildlife. On the day I'm recounting, I was sitting in a ground blind in a wooded area that branched out from the wood line, with fields on either side. Behind me, there was a swale—which is a sunken, marshy piece of land—and to my left, roughly twenty yards (18 m) away, was a small ravine with a creek flowing through the bottom and a gradual slope downwards. The ravine ran parallel to the north wall of my blind but curved slightly before leveling out to the east.

My blind is octagonal and has four windows, little flaps with latches to keep them up in the "closed" position. It was situated such that every window faced a cardinal direction. Primarily, I was sitting facing east, farther into the woods, with the road directly behind me, a good 130 yards (119 m) back or so.

The door to enter the blind was behind me to the left. At this point, the wind had increased and was blowing from the north, so I closed that window. I always kept the window facing the road closed for firearm safety.

THERE WAS NO HUMAN, NOR ANIMAL, NOTHING STANDING WHERE I HAD HEARD THESE FOOTSTEPS.

After sitting in the blind for about two hours that morning, without so much as a squirrel sighting, I heard footsteps. Or at least, leaves crunching and what sounded like footsteps. It was behind me, slightly to the left. It struck me as a little odd because it sounded too close, like I should have been hearing it sooner. I figured it must have been coming up from the swale behind me. Since it was a popular area for deer to bed down, I prepared myself to take a shot once it came into view.

However, I couldn't risk turning around and making noise. Opening the windows would also frighten the deer away. But this wasn't a deer. It sounded like human strides and were a bit too heavy to be a deer. I wasn't immediately concerned; I guessed my father was checking on me or something, but he absolutely would have called or texted me before making a hike from his blind to mine.

Then I thought, maybe another friend of ours whom we frequently hunt with was coming to check the blind; I was right near his tree stand, after all. I even wondered if this was a certain game warden, who had been very active this season. Either way, the footsteps seemed to come right to the door of my blind, maybe four feet (1 m) back from it.

Assuming it was a person, I reached over and unlatched a window to catch a glimpse outside, as opening the door of the blind was an arduous task in the darkness. When I looked outside the blind, I saw, to my surprise, absolutely nothing. There was no human, nor animal, nothing standing where I had heard these footsteps.

Deciding I was simply freaking myself out over nothing, I closed the window again and got situated back in my chair. A few seconds later, the footsteps started once more. They walked past the door and were directly to my left.

One must wonder how many times the older gentleman had walked those paths, how deep his soles had dug into the mud and mire. Like a shoe against the ground, his energy leaving behind an imprint of its own.

A residual haunting is not a ghost, but a vivid replay of a past event. It resembles a haunting "recording" that can play repeatedly, revealing the story in the same precise manner every time. The individual involved in a residual haunting remains completely oblivious and unaffected by your presence. It's as if you are merely an observer, as there is no spirit or ghost involved, only the lingering echo of a bygone occurrence.

They were clear as day, no question about it. Outside my blind, I heard the rustling of something moving. I quickly reached over and opened the window again, hoping to catch a glimpse of whoever or whatever had made the noise. But no person, no animal, nothing. Shock ran through me.

The footsteps had sounded no more than three feet (1 m) from me. I should have been able to touch whatever was outside if I had poked my arm out the window and waved it around. How could I not see anything?

Thoroughly spooked, I got chills and closed that window, sitting back down and waiting. Sure enough, the footsteps picked up again. They walked forward but didn't go far enough that they entered my vision. They veered off to the left, away from me, heading northeast. I didn't even bother trying to look this time. Not right away, at least. After a few seconds, I heard them begin down the slope into the ravine and walk right down to the creek at the base. Leaning forward in my blind, I peered in that direction and glimpsed where they were coming from, but whatever it was remained hidden in the ravine. The footsteps got down to a particular section of the creek, stopped, and I never heard them again.

At that moment, my mind was racing with thoughts.

"What was that?"

"Was that real?"

"Is it still down there?"

But then I realized something. It was roughly eight years ago that my friend's father passed away. I had had a strong bond with this man and frequently thought of him while hunting. In fact, the tree stand I was near had belonged to him. After his death and cremation, we had spread his ashes in the very creek where I heard the footsteps vanish.

Suddenly, I knew exactly whom I heard. I knew the old hoot was checking who was in the blind. I'm sure he was happy to see the "young blood," as he liked to call me, sitting there, keeping the tradition going. Not all ghost experiences have to be scary or malicious. Some can even be comforting. For me, this one certainly was.

THE HORROR AT THE EDGE
OF THE FOREST

The machinations of two young explorers lead them to a building
under construction. No matter your age or state of physical fitness,
when it comes time to fight for your life, you better fight like hell.

FIELD NOTES

Location: A rural location in the Deep South, USA
Date/Time: A July evening, at sunset
Atmosphere: Childlike curiosity, filled with the promise of summer vacation

I grew up in a densely wooded area in the Deep South. The kind that would have
miles of nothing but gigantic trees packed tight on both sides of the road before
you'd ever see a house.

I lived in a small neighborhood of fifteen houses that made up four streets off the
main road. However, it didn't bother me much because it meant I always had a playmate
since we were the only children around for miles. During the summer, it felt like there
was always a group of kids running through backyards to visit each other's houses
during the day. When the sun set, you would see those same kids rushing off home trying
to beat the streetlights coming on.

On one particularly cool July afternoon, just as the sun was setting, I was sitting at
the top of the steepest of the streets in our neighborhood and looking at the little dirt
road at the bottom. I was with my best friend Danny and we were waiting for the cars
that we knew were down there to leave.

Workers were building two new houses at the end of this dirt road, about 150 yards (137 m) from the main road. And seeing how Danny and I wanted to build a new fort, we needed supplies.

We both assumed that there would be an abundance of scrap wood and nails lying around, and we thought it wouldn't matter if we took some things that were going to be thrown away. The problem was, we had been sitting there for almost an hour already and had seen no one come down that dirt road and turn to leave.

Finally, after what felt like an eternity of sitting in the same spot staring at the same dirt road that disappeared behind the same stand of way-too-tall trees, I'd had enough. I stood up and told Danny to come on because I figured they must have already left before we got there.

The sky was completely devoid of light, and I was angry with myself for delaying my departure on the dirt road. However, I had been confident that I had witnessed the workers leaving around the same time just before sunset every day that week. Worst-case scenario, we'd jump behind some trees on the side of the road if we saw headlights coming down the road.

It took maybe five minutes to walk down that dirt road, but it was dark and the light from the flashlight Danny had somehow thought to bring didn't really do much to light up the dirt road. If anything, it made the shadows on the sides of the road look way darker than they should have been. But we finally entered the big clearing that the workers had cut out of the trees for the houses under construction.

Anyone initially entering the clearing would see that the houses were standing opposite each other, about forty yards (37 m) apart. It appeared that additional houses would be constructed nearby in the future, but what caught my attention was the nearly completed house with lights on inside and a truck parked beside it.

Danny and I had already stopped, searching for any sign of someone inside, perhaps working late or packing up their tools to take home for the weekend, as some of these guys had a lot to pack up.

We didn't hear anyone, though. There was no one walking about, no one stepping outside with tools or loading items into the truck. Without realizing it, we had already snuck right up to the house and were standing in front of the open, doorless entryway with its makeshift steps that looked like they shouldn't have been able to support the weight of a full-grown man going up and down them, much less ten-year-old me.

Either way, I slowly crept up the steps, just far enough to poke my head inside and look around. I had a clear view of most of the house since they hadn't installed Sheetrock in many areas, and I didn't spot anyone inside.

I jumped back down the steps and told Danny that the guy must have left his truck there and rode with someone else. Maybe he'd come back for it later, but we needed to hurry because our moms would already be mad that we took so long to get home from playing outside.

We quickly began searching through the enormous pile of wood that someone had thrown out beside the house, hoping to find sizeable pieces that we could use for walls. After gathering and testing the small load of scrap wood for weight to ensure it wasn't too heavy to carry, we continued our search.

I found what I was looking for, but it wasn't a small box of nails. Instead, I discovered a big metal Folger's coffee can that looked like someone had been putting any leftover loose nails or screws into it. I quickly stuffed a bunch of items into the front pocket of my shirt and headed toward the door. Suddenly, I heard Danny fall behind me. I turned around and saw him lying in what looked like paint that someone had forgotten to clean up after they spilled it. I laughed a little and gave him a hand up—and that was when we heard it.

Someone was walking around outside. But it didn't really sound right. It sounded slower. Each step sounded deliberate, as if the person outside already knew we were inside and intentionally walked around the back of the house to make their presence known.

We panicked and quickly ran out the front, jumping down the steps and sprinting away, abandoning the small stack of wood we had gathered. We raced toward the area among the trees where the dirt road led back to the safety of our neighborhood, guided by the comforting glow of streetlights that would light our path back home.

The problem was, whoever had been behind the house walking slowly around was now to the right of us, just far enough into the trees that I could only make out

We've all heard of the horrors involved with the Salem Witch Trials. But before innocent women in America were accused of witchcraft and burnt at the stake, Europe was experiencing its own bout of paranoia. These werewolf trials, also known as lycanthropy trials, were a dark chapter in European history.

Between the fifteenth and seventeenth centuries, folklore and superstition were rich with tales of werewolves, beings that could transform into wolves or wolflike creatures. Accusations of werewolf-ism often emerged from a combination of fear, rumors, and a desire to explain unexplained phenomena. Confessions were often extracted through intense interrogations, which frequently involved torture. The punishments were meant to be both horrifying and a deterrent to others.

The case of Peter Stumpp is exceptionally gruesome, involving the forced removal of his skin and his body being burned at the stake. His severed head, displayed to the public as a wolflike entity, served as a chilling reminder of the punishment awaiting those accused of engaging in supernatural acts or affiliating with the Devil.

his shadow. But his shadow looked funny to me. While sprinting toward the end of the road, I would quickly glance to my right in search of the shadow. However, it would suddenly dart off to our left, getting closer. Close enough, I could see that it wasn't a man.

It was too tall to be a man.

Never had I encountered a man whose ears stuck out and curved backwards, forming a distinct point just behind his head, unmistakably resembling the head of a werewolf. The creature had a long snout and eyes that faintly glowed a dull green, but it remained shrouded in shadows as I ran in fear, unable to discern its full appearance.

The thing was big, though. My God, it was huge. The thing, partially concealed in shadows and slightly hunched over, was significantly taller than my dad at six foot three (190 cm).

We were almost at the end when this thing was suddenly behind us. In the blink of an eye, it went from being beside us to suddenly lurking right behind us. So impossibly close, I thought it was going to grab me at any moment and rip me to shreds.

Just then, I remembered why my shirt felt heavy and was flopping up and down as I ran for my life. The nails in my front pocket! As I was running, I swiftly reached in and dropped what I could behind me.

My confidence in it being too large to notice my presence quickly wavered when a yelping, snarling sound filled the air with unmistakable pain. A crashing noise, which I desperately hoped meant the creature had fallen. Then the yelp. I couldn't believe my luck. It had stepped on the nails.

Just then, Danny and I burst through the tree line, panting, as we started running up the street. Maybe a little slower, but still we pushed on up the steep road to the top before we stopped underneath the bright glow of the streetlight.

Looking down at the trees we had just run through, I couldn't help but notice the spot—the very spot that could have taken away my last breath. It was standing outside the trees. We could see it clearly, and it frightened me to the very core of my being.

That one moment filled me with unprecedented terror. I believed it would follow us down the street, knowing it had been toying with us previously. I knew it was much faster than it had been. I knew I had gotten lucky with the nails and that if this thing ran after us, it would certainly catch us in a matter of seconds.

Despite my fears, nothing happened. It's like this thing took one step back and then the trees, or maybe the darkness itself, just swallowed it up again. It was gone, and I was damn near crying tears of relief as we turned and ran up my walkway to the front door of my house. We ran straight to my room and closed my window as my mom shouted after us, asking where in the world we had been.

We said nothing to my mom and dad about what had happened. I mean, come on, they were not going to believe a couple of kids just ran from a freaking werewolf, anyway.

We didn't sleep at all that night because we were way too scared that thing was going to come out of the woods behind my house and get us. But as night wore on, the sun finally came up again. I mustered the courage to look outside the window, but there was nothing there. Or at least I thought there was nothing.

As I looked and the sun shone on the ground outside my window, I could see prints in the soft earth.

Big, huge paw prints.

This thing, this werewolf, had been at my window during the night.

It was clearly certain that it was my window because when I stepped outside that morning and observed, mine was the lone window with paw prints beneath it.

I freaked out and went inside, but I stopped in the living room because I could hear my parents' hushed whispers from the kitchen. I snuck a little closer to the doorway, going into the kitchen so I could hear what they were saying.

My dad's friend, who was a police officer, had stumbled upon a man's dead body that morning. This occurred after they promptly responded to a distress call from the wife of one of the men who had been working on the house my friend and I had entered the day before. She expressed concern about her husband's failure to return home from work the previous night. The situation was unusual since, for twenty-seven years, the man had consistently arrived home before nine on Fridays.

So, when she called for the fifth time throughout the night, the police finally went to the worksite just after dawn and discovered that the guy's truck was still there. They had found blood inside the house, and I instantly knew that Danny hadn't slipped on the paint after all. It must have been that guy's blood. We had concentrated so much on just getting out of there alive that we hadn't thought to check.

They didn't find his body right away. At least, not all of it. They discovered his legs right on the outskirts of the trees behind the house, and they found his head close to his legs.

But the rest of him . . .

The rest of him they found in a tree about fifty yards (45 m) from the house. The creature had taken him up the tree with the intention of consuming him gradually, and it seemed to have left him there upon hearing our presence as we investigated the house.

The werewolf trials of Pierre Burgot and Michel Verdun in 1521 were part of a larger wave of witch-hunting and persecution that swept across Europe during the early modern period. The inquisitors, acting on behalf of the Pope, were determined to root out any supposed practitioners of witchcraft and other supernatural activities.

In their confessions, Burgot and Verdun detailed a horrifying pact they had made with the Devil, where they exchanged their souls for sustenance. They claimed to have encountered a mysterious man in black who provided them with an ointment capable of transforming them into werewolves. This transformation supposedly allowed them to attend midnight gatherings with witches, where they engaged in sinister rituals and hunted down innocent children to satisfy their monstrous cravings. Despite their confessions, the trials were highly controversial, with some questioning the veracity of the accusations and the reliability of the confessions extracted under torture. Nevertheless, Burgot and Verdun, including a third man who refused to confess, were ultimately convicted of their alleged crimes and sentenced to death by burning at the stake. This dark chapter in history serves as a reminder of the intense fear and paranoia surrounding supernatural beliefs during that time.

After that, our parents didn't really let us do much. The rest of the summer was spent indoors, but I was fine with that. Because I knew it wasn't a mountain lion or a bear that killed that man and dragged his half-eaten torso twenty-five feet (8 m) up a tree. It was a werewolf, and it knew where I lived. It had stood outside my window for God knows how long. Why didn't it kill me?

These things, these beasts, are real.

And there, just outside, skulking around, waiting for someone to slip up.

And come too close.

GHOST STORIES

The afterlife is a mystery, but ghost stories are everywhere. Some deny fearing death, but I believe it is natural to fear it. Fear of death is really fear of the unknown. We don't know what awaits us when the long dark takes hold.

Ghost stories are the most abundant type of submission I receive. It seems everyone knows someone who has had a ghostly encounter. Hundreds of ghost-hunting teams in the US and UK search for contact with the deceased.

When dealing with spirits, caution is advised, as not all ghosts may be remnants of the living. Some are evil spirits, ancient things that seek to deceive and torment those who dare to call out to them. Some call them demons, and they seem to appear in almost every culture around the world.

The stories in this section feature intangible entities that haunt us directly or otherwise. Ghosts or demons, there's no way to tell. So, be careful what speaks to you from beyond. It's not always a good idea to speak back.

SUPERSTITION OR REALITY?

It's said we never know our true appearance. That mirrors
warp and flip our image, showing us a false reality, and allowing us
to see into a world that very well may be peering back.

FIELD NOTES

Location: Agoo, La Union, Philippines
Date/Time: July, on a summer vacation far from home
Atmosphere: A creeping horror of something lurking just beyond your perception

Right before my family immigrated to the United States from the Philippines, it was
decided that I would spend an entire year with my mother's side of the family while the
international move and paperwork were being sorted out. These relatives lived in the
northern part of the archipelago, in a very rural area called Agoo, La Union. All around
the area were rice paddies and tree lines that housed fishponds, which also transitioned
to more rice paddies surrounding the area. The home itself was two hours away by foot
from the beach if you cut through the rice paddies.

I had visited them before and enjoyed being there. The houses in this area were
built in the Spanish colonial style and were made almost entirely of some red-colored
hardwood and furniture that looked as though someone had made them specifically to
match the house. It felt scenic and more relaxing than the modern city life to which I
was accustomed. However, my grandparents and the family that lived there had one rule:

"Do not open a specific room on the second floor; and if you somehow find it open, do
not remove the cover of the mirror in there."

I had never questioned this rule before, but now, with a whole year at my disposal, and being ten years old, I couldn't help but wonder.

I spent about six months curious, but nothing unusual happened. When I passed the room, I would end up staring at the door. I would ask my grandparents about it, but they would just smile at me and tell me to ignore it. My grandparents are a blend of Spanish, Japanese, and Filipino heritage, so they hold many superstitions stemming from multiple cultures. I excused the rule as superstition. The rest of the family told me to ignore it as well, but emphasized avoiding the room.

Three months before our flight to the United States, things changed. One July afternoon, I had spent the day with the local kids climbing trees trying to gather Java plums—getting bitten by large red ants as a result—since everyone else was away doing errands and business.

I believe it was around 4 or 5 p.m. when I went back to the house, as my grandparents and cousins were coming home. I ran upstairs to grab a change of clothes and a towel since I had spent most of the day sweaty and dirty. When I turned right from the top of the stairs, I entered an open area that resembled a second living room. Sofas were arranged along three walls, and the open windows provided a gentle breeze. I don't remember opening them before I left the house to play.

There were two doors in that area. If you continued straight from the doorway after turning right from the top of the stairs, you would find the doors on your left. The door farther from the stairs opened to the room where I kept my clothes. The closest door to the stairs was supposed to be kept locked. Well, when I went through the doorway, the door was wide open.

It was the smallest room I have ever seen. It was almost like a closet, maybe slightly wider to fit a twin XL bed on the left side; but there wasn't anything in that room, except a mirror at the very back. At this moment, I am five foot eleven (180 cm), and that item would have been a minimum of six foot four (193 cm), with the wooden frame and everything. The mirror itself was oval-shaped, which I didn't know at the time because there was a thick white cloth covering the whole thing.

From ancient times to the present day, people have held various beliefs and customs when it comes to storing and interacting with mirrors. In some cultures, it is believed that a mirror can capture and hold the souls of those who gaze into it, leading to the practice of covering mirrors in homes during times of mourning.

Other cultures view mirrors as portals to the spirit world, and caution against looking into them at night for fear of summoning unwanted entities. Additionally, some traditions advise against placing mirrors directly opposite doorways or beds, as it is believed to invite bad luck or restless spirits.

I felt drawn to it, but I remembered I was not supposed to go in there. The longer I stared, the more uneasy I felt. I told myself to look to see if there was anyone home, but my body wouldn't move.

I was standing a few feet away from the entrance of that room. My mind went racing. I knew I didn't see anyone on my way to the house or on my way up. The more I realized this, the more the hairs at the back of my neck stood up.

Out of nowhere, someone grabbed my arm, and I screamed in panic. I saw my grandmother, frightened and concerned, and there was also a hint of anger in her gaze. She moved her body so that it obscured the view of the mirror and asked me in a very stern voice, "Did you look in the mirror?"

I looked around, a bit confused. It was already dark outside but, in my mind, there was still light. I had only gone up a few minutes ago. I told her I didn't know, that I had just got back in from playing. While guiding me downstairs, she apologized for their late arrival due to a problem at the rice-hulling facility where my family harvested rice. When I looked at the clock downstairs, it was almost 8 p.m.

I guess she might have told my grandfather and my cousins because they all went upstairs together while I was eating dinner. I didn't do anything after that, as I was still confused. By the time I went upstairs to sleep, the door was closed.

They had attached something by the doorknob and looped a chain through it, taut to prevent the door from swinging inward and opening. That confused me even more since that still meant someone from the outside could undo the chains, but I guess they didn't think I was the one who opened the door in the first place.

Aside from my grandparents and the room where I kept my clothes, which only had one bed for my female cousin, the rest of us slept on bamboo mats with a futon on top that we rolled out on the floor of the living room–like area upstairs. There were four of us, ranging from ten to fifteen in age; I was the youngest. My mind was preoccupied that night, and I couldn't sleep until sunrise. I only slept an hour or two before my cousins woke me up, but nothing had occurred.

For an entire week, it was peaceful, and I had forgotten all about it.

Then things picked up. Exactly a week after, during an evening just after dinner, we were all watching a show and I had to use the restroom. While I was on the toilet, I felt a chill. My senses were prickling as I felt watched from all directions. I tried my best to act like nothing was happening.

Telling myself not to turn around or look up, I sat there, nerves causing my body to shiver. As I wiped, a sound startled me, causing me to bite my lip until it bled. I tried to suppress a scream. I heard a rhythmic noise, like someone was clicking their tongue. Each sound clicked in threes, separated by two seconds, and grew louder each time.

I pushed the bidet multiple times and re-wiped as fast as I could and ran out. I had forgotten to pull my pants up. It was a miracle I didn't trip, but my eldest male cousin, Eugene, looked at me worriedly. Everyone had gone up to bed while I was on the toilet. Apparently, I had taken too long.

The other family members had asked Eugene to wait for me downstairs. I couldn't explain what had happened to me in the bathroom to him, but it must have spooked him because he looked out the windows before shutting them. Unlike your typical windows made of a single pane of glass, these windows were small, rectangular sheets of glass that lined up horizontally like horizontal blinds, and they closed similarly. He urged me upstairs after shutting them and did the same to the windows upstairs before we lay down to sleep.

THE FOOTSTEPS ON THE CEILING STOPPED RIGHT ABOVE ME, BUT I COULD FEEL THAT IF I OPENED MY EYES, SOMETHING WOULD BE STARING RIGHT AT ME, AND IT MADE ME WANT TO SCREAM.

It was extremely dark; it must have been very late at night. My sleep was disrupted by the sound of creaking. I was right next to Eugene, who was the closest to the door and, by extension, the stairs. I could tell the creaking was coming from the door because, in the pitch-black darkness, a faint glow emitted from it, gradually intensifying, until the creaking sound shifted to the floorboards.

I felt a pinch on my arm; it was Eugene facing me. I could barely see his face in the dark, but the moonlight coming through the now-opened room made some of his features visible. He looked scared, his head shaking side to side as though telling me not to look.

The finger on his lips signaled me to stay quiet. He closed his eyes for several seconds, then opened them, telling me to do the same by nodding. We didn't exchange any words, but the widening of his eyes when the creak of the floorboards sounded louder and closer made it obvious. I began to sweat, my chest heaving, but I forced myself not to make a sound and closed my eyes.

The creak continued moving around the room. Eugene gripped my arm to make sure I was still there since he had closed his eyes. I kept my eyes shut, but the anxiety of the creaking sound approaching and receding caused me to tense up, and my eyelids started to ache.

I don't know how long it took; it felt eternal. The emergence of clear taps followed the absence of footsteps on the floors, on the ceiling, almost resembling distorted footsteps. A loud metallic creak filled the room, coming from the farthest wall.

My eyes were closed, but my back was pointing against the source of the metallic creak. The cool breeze informed me that someone had opened the window. The taps on the ceiling were right above me. Eugene's hand tightened, and I got a feeling my other cousins were also awake.

The footsteps on the ceiling stopped right above me, but I could feel that if I opened my eyes, something would be staring right at me, and it made me want to scream. I could feel the breeze from the now-open window against my back, and there was a stiff brush against my cheek. The rhythmic tongue clicks returned, louder this time, as if the source knew we were now fully awake. The sound of something hollow tapping on the opened glass pane, taunting us, came from behind me.

Right by our heads, a sofa separated us from the wall. The two windows on the wall right above us creaked. The pungent smell of tobacco assaulted my senses, followed by the sharp scents of sulfur and ammonia. From that same window, I could hear heavy breathing each time the tobacco smell surged. The leaves of the mango tree by that window shook like something was moving the branches.

The tongue clicks behind me, the smell of the tobacco, sulfur, and ammonia, as well as the heavy breathing right by my head continued forever. I wasn't in the right mind to keep track of time, but I knew for sure that it would be a while before the floorboard creaked again.

I heard cackling from both directions out the window, then felt an unmistakable icy hand grasping my right ankle. Eugene squeezed my arm; I guess he could feel me become more tense. I tried to relax, but I had peed myself.

I don't know what happened after. I know I spent the entire night awake. When the chickens of the neighbor cawed, Eugene sat up, followed by the rest of my cousins. They were all drenched in sweat, and so was I. They would have surely made fun of me for peeing my pants, but they didn't.

It was still just before sunrise, but the soft glow of dawn allowed us to navigate with ease. We turned on the lights and ran downstairs as a group. The locked room was wide open, and the mirror had no covers.

When I came around to look sometime later that day, the windowpanes had scratch marks that weren't there before. The ceiling had scratch marks too. My uncle and Eugene were trying to fix the door. Apparently, someone completely wrecked the knob, so I could see inside while they were trying to fix it. When I first looked in the room, the floor by the mirror was pristine, without a single scratch. Now, it was covered in deep gouges.

This experience would continue with differing intensity for the rest of the time I was there, especially the feeling of being watched.

That feeling stopped for a long while since moving to the United States until I remembered it all recently. Since then, I feel creeped out at night, especially when I'm alone. I wonder if my memory has been altered by the countless books on the paranormal I've read since then, causing me to be overly cautious. However, the sensation of being observed has continued.

I don't know anymore. Is it just suggestive superstition or is it all real?

One of the most popular stories surrounding mirrors is that of Bloody Mary, a supernatural entity known for appearing in mirrors when summoned.

There are many backstories for the legend, but the most plausible one takes place in the 1800s. Mary was a young girl who fell ill during the 1800s. In those times, people often mistakenly pronounced others dead, which led to the practice of placing a bell in the coffin to alert others if the person woke up. When Mary "died," her parents left the house, and a neighbor, unaware of her potential survival, began filling her grave. Mary woke up, pulled the string attached to the bell, but no one heard it. She desperately tried to escape her coffin, but ultimately died. Her spirit is now attached to mirrors. It is believed that saying "Bloody Mary" three times in front of a mirror will cause her to harm the person who summoned her.

NEVER OPEN YOUR DOOR FOR THE LATE TRICK-OR-TREATER

Kids trot around dressed as ghouls and monsters in search
of candy. It's not all about the treats, though. Sometimes you'll
be on the cruel end of a trick. Hook, line, and sinker.

FIELD NOTES

Location: A charming residential neighborhood in a typical suburb
Date/Time: All Hallows' Eve
Atmosphere: Mischievously crafty, sinisterly festive

In my neighborhood, it's an unspoken rule that Halloween trick-or-treating ends at
10 p.m. Usually, the kids walking around come at different times, depending on their
age. The cute little four- to seven-year-olds come earliest when it is still light out. They
are probably my favorite. Then come the older kids; they are kind of awkward and silly.
Finally, the kids who are self-conscious about still trick-or-treating, usually high school
freshmen and sophomores. They are the best for pranking, so I enjoy that a lot.

Anyway, this particular Halloween died down around 9:50 p.m., and I retired to my
couch with the leftover candy. Outside, the sound of kids faded as they deserted the
streets one by one, signaling the end of Halloween. I fell asleep around midnight. The
surrounding area was a graveyard of Jolly Rancher wrappers and lollipop sticks.

A timid rap on the door woke me up.

I sat up, half asleep. My mind was too foggy to be sure, but I think I asked who it was.
The next knock was much louder and shook the cobwebs from my brain. I jumped off the
couch and cautiously approached the door.

I WATCHED IN HORROR AS FISHHOOKS PROTRUDED EVERYWHERE FROM HIS BODY.

Through the peephole, I caught a glimpse of a small boy dressed in a surprisingly sharply tailored suit. It was perfectly ironed and inky black. The boy's face was pale and smooth, with a vibrant blush on his rounded cheeks. The most stunning part, however, was his piercing, bright blue eyes.

I opened the door and greeted the kid. I asked him what he was doing up so late and where his parents were. He replied he was hungry and wanted candy, ignoring my second question. I hesitantly brought the candy bowl to him. He fished through the candy and dug his hand to the bottom. He felt around for a while, never looking into the bowl. I found this odd but didn't say anything.

Suddenly, the kid screamed and pulled his hand out of the bowl. It was bleeding fiercely. I freaked out and grabbed paper towels and tried to wipe away the blood. But the kid kept screaming and slapping my hand away. He gave me a haunting, accusing stare with those deep blue eyes.

He pointed at me and yelled, with tears running down his cheeks. With a furious scream, he declared that my efforts were in vain, and now I would face the price. I did not know what he was trying to say. As I saw the fishhook in the boy's hand, I suspected that it was a ploy to falsely accuse me and sue me for money.

But the kid kept screaming and bleeding an inhuman amount.

His eyes went wide, and he started screaming even more frantically. He grabbed his arms and swatted all over his body like there were bees attacking him. I watched in horror as fishhooks protruded everywhere from his body. My porch was now a puddle of blood. I slammed the door, and within a few minutes, the screaming ended. I wondered how no one had heard the kid screaming, and I hoped desperately that it was all some twisted hallucination.

I fell asleep much later that night. When I woke up, I felt extremely refreshed. The sun was glowing; it seemed like a good morning. The events of the previous night were just a vague memory, like a dream. In fact, I am almost convinced it was one. When I stepped outside, there was no puddle of blood. None of the neighbors said anything about hearing a screaming child in the middle of the night.

But there is one thing that keeps me from setting it aside as a dream. Halfway through the day, I realized I had been clutching something in my hand. When I looked, it was a small, rusty fishhook.

During ancient times, there was a belief that the boundary separating our world and the spirit realm grew weakest on Samhain (Halloween). This meant that the spirits of the departed could freely interact with the living. According to superstition, these visiting spirits had the ability to assume human appearances, often disguising themselves as beggars, and would go door-to-door during Samhain, seeking money or food. However, if you were to turn them away without offering any assistance, you risked incurring the wrath of these spirits, potentially leading to curses or haunting experiences.

Perhaps this boy was nothing more than a traveling spirit, looking to play one more prank before the veil closed again.

WHY I DON'T GO INTO HOSPITAL MORGUES ANYMORE

Working so closely with the dead might lead you to believe
that the afterlife isn't so frightening. But what about when you're
reminded that the dead can still affect the living?

FIELD NOTES

Location: The hospital morgue, anywhere
Date/Time: During the dead shift
Atmosphere: A chilling stillness

My profession revolves around funeral care, so I guess it's no surprise I have a story like this. I work for a company that handles the transportation of bodies from the place of passing to the funeral home for preparation and storage. I've been in this job for many years now, and honestly, I love it. My role in helping others during what is often one of the hardest and darkest moments in their lives means so much to me.

One of the most common runs I find myself on is going to hospital morgues, taking out as many bodies as possible, and delivering them to be embalmed or cremated at the many funeral homes around the state.

I've been to the hospital in this story so many times that I knew most of the security guards by name. The guard who came to meet me, whom I'll call Jed, escorted me through the winding halls and mazelike labyrinth that seem to make up the lower levels of most hospitals.

Everything was as normal. We talked about our lives, how work was treating us, and swapped stories of the baffling experiences that these jobs will occasionally bestow upon us. When we got to the morgue, I went through the usual procedures: sign documentation, draw up ankle tags, put on gloves, and confirm all the bodies are exactly who they're supposed to be.

Typically, Jed and I stay together the whole time in case I need any help to move someone and to make sure that everything is locked up again when I leave. This time, though, Jed received a call on his radio about an angry woman who had just attempted to assault a nurse for telling her something she didn't like.

Jed told me he had to go and that he'd be back as soon as possible. He rushed off and left me alone in the cooler. I didn't mind. Some people find being alone with dead bodies a very unnerving experience, always weary of the haunting look of their glazed-over eyes—but not me.

I enjoy talking to bodies, venting about my day, entrusting important secrets, or just simply telling them how good my lunch sounds. All of which fall onto ears that can never again retell the words I impart to them.

As I was detailing the lunch I would have as soon as I got back to the van, I noticed a sound. It sounded like someone brushing against the plastic of the body bags that they stored the bodies in. I looked around the room, expecting Jed to maybe have returned and try to startle me like he had done numerous times before. There was no one else in the room, so I chalked it up to one of the fans rustling some of the plastic. I moved the first body without issue, but when I went to pull out the second one, I heard that sound again.

It sounded just like someone adjusting the plastic shrouds, but quietly, like they were trying to keep me from noticing it. I decided to just load up this last body and then leave, whether or not Jed was back. I opened the bag to compare my ankle tag with the one the hospitals put on the toe, when the lights began to flicker, and the fans began to pulse and shudder.

It lasted for a long moment, then everything suddenly went dark, and the silence was deafening. In surprise, I cursed and then slowly shuffled my way across the dark, cold room. I froze in my tracks when the silence was disrupted by a quiet sound, amplified by the room's silence.

If anywhere is going to be haunted, it'll be a hospital. As fresh bodies are moved and prodded, spirits linger around the morgue.

The infamous hospital that was known as the Pennsylvania State Lunatic Asylum until 1937 has a long and eerie history that contributes to its reputation as one of the most haunted places in the state. Visitors and staff have reported hearing blood-curdling screams and strange noises, not to mention seeing shadows and ghostly apparitions. The morgue, basement, and hidden tunnels are said to be the epicenter of these encounters. Witnesses have reported the sudden appearance of blood-like stains in the morgue's exam room. These occurrences have attracted curious individuals who want to experience the chilling presence for themselves.

The sound of a zipper slowly unzipping from the back of the room.

I internally screamed at my body to get to the door, to put as much distance between me and the sound as possible. But it refused to listen, the unnerving sound of the zipper cementing me in place. After a long, tense moment, the sound ceased. My mind was racing to come up with an explanation for this sound. Was this a prank? Perhaps another sound, just misinterpreted in this dark room?

Another sound interrupted my panicked thoughts: plastic shifting, and then the slap of something smacking onto the floor. Control rushed back into my body as I heard footsteps slowly smacking, one after another, on the hard concrete floor. It was coming closer to me. I ran across the room, desperate to find the door and escape this chilled prison, but the room seemed longer than it should have been.

The farther I ran, the faster and closer the footsteps sounded. Just as the footsteps seemed to put whatever was chasing me just a few feet behind me, my feet seemed to just fly out from beneath me. I fell to the floor with a painful thud, and once again, all sound ceased.

IT SOUNDED JUST LIKE SOMEONE ADJUSTING THE PLASTIC SHROUDS, BUT QUIETLY, LIKE THEY WERE TRYING TO KEEP ME FROM NOTICING IT.

I lay there for what felt like an eternity, trying to catch my breath, waiting to hear something, anything, that would tell me where the source of the sound was. The dark and cold were the only things my body could register for a few moments before I realized the sensation of something hovering inches from my face.

Once again, my body froze in terror at what unseen horror had placed itself in front of me. I felt an icy breath exhale onto my face, the stench of decay and death briefly overloading my senses, as the wet sound of a mouth slowly opening began.

I felt whatever it was leaning closer toward me, just about to touch me, as the door to the cooler burst open, and it suddenly flooded the room with light and the sound of fans whirring ceaselessly. Jed!

Seeing me sprawled across the floor, pale and breathless, with a body lying on the other side of the room, Jed gave me a look of alarm as he asked me if everything was okay. I told him I just tripped and fell as I was coming out to get him to help me pick up a body that I had accidentally dropped. He laughed at me as we picked up and returned the fallen body to its crypt table. I loaded up my last body and bolted out and away from that hospital.

I don't know what happened in that room—whether it was a hallucination or if I was a witness to some kind of paranormal encounter. I still work this job, and I still go to hospitals all over the state, but suffice it to say, I don't go into any morgue coolers by myself anymore.

CYNTHIA

With all the houses we walk by daily, it's only natural to wonder what goes on in them. What sorts of people live there? Do they watch TV? Prefer warm or cool light? What horrors lurk beyond the doors we may never open?

FIELD NOTES

Location: The outskirts of town, somewhere in the South, USA
Date/Time: The dead of night, summer of 2021
Atmosphere: Eerily silent, until you hear distant laughter

I'm a young police officer in a Southern city. As a child, it was my dream to become a police officer. I made tinfoil badges and carved sticks to look like pistols. I took reports with crayons and chased imaginary criminals. Twenty years later, well into my job, I average three hours of sleep and have grueling anxiety attacks. Like my peers, I've seen terrible things. It's what we signed up for, so I don't expect sympathy.

But out of all the horrible things I've seen and witnessed, my trauma comes from 2021, when I responded to a call that haunts me every second.

It was around 3 a.m. I was typing a larceny report in my car while the show *Ozark* played in the background. The night shift was shorthanded, so my typical beat partner wasn't working. Dispatch requested me for a welfare check, which is when you are asked to ensure that someone is safe and sound. Welfare checks are usually harmless, although it's when you're more likely to find dead bodies. The reporting party is usually a family member who couldn't get hold of the person.

I received the information and started driving. They tasked me with checking the welfare of an elderly woman named Cynthia who lived alone on the outskirts of town,

NOT A GIGGLE, BUT DELIRIOUS, GUT-BUSTING LAUGHTER FROM WHAT SOUNDED LIKE AN OLD LADY.

barely within city limits. Her granddaughter lived a few states away and hadn't heard from her. She assumed her grandma accidentally switched her cellphone to silent, as she often did.

Dispatch usually sends two officers, but every now and again, they'll give an officer an option to take the call alone. Because of staffing levels and the nature of the call, I handled it myself. Worst-case scenario, granny bit the dust, and I would call a medical examiner to work an unattended death.

I drove a good fifteen minutes to the residence. There were no other houses in the area. It was so quiet that the sound of gravel under my tires was thunderous. Beyond the mailbox was a locked gate and a long dirt driveway.

I had no desire to walk that driveway alone, in the dark, without my patrol car. My hand instinctively went for the radio, but I decided against calling for another officer. I would've looked silly asking for another after committing to doing it solo. Plus, it would have been an even longer drive for them. I manned up, jumped the gate, and made what turned out to be the worst decision of my life.

If it wasn't for the moonlight, the darkness would have been so deep that I couldn't even make out my own feet. Law enforcement training had taught me to be tactical with my flashlight. I'd only use it in short bursts. It was a good way to be sneaky.

I finally reached the house and stood in front of it. It was an old wooden home with two stories. Every window was pitch-black besides one on the second floor. It had a purple curtain with white stripes. I stepped onto the unstable wraparound porch and listened carefully.

There was nothing but absolute silence. No TV, no creaks, no fans. Everything was still. I tentatively knocked and announced myself. There was no answer and no noise. I knocked even louder and announced again—still nothing.

I stepped off the porch to reevaluate the situation. Once far enough, I looked up to the second story. The light was off. Normally, I wouldn't find something like that unsettling, but an eerie feeling washed over me, heightening my senses. Since the light was off, I couldn't see whether someone was looking back at me. I had a terrifying feeling that they were. I grabbed my flashlight and shined it on the window. No one was standing there, but the curtain had moved and was still swaying.

I went back to the door and knocked even louder. My voice filled the night, disrupting the silence. I explained loudly who I was and which police department I was with.

For several minutes, I stood there waiting for any sign of life. I was ready to hightail it back to the road, but figured I'd wait another minute. I had done my job. My purpose for being there was to verify she was still alive. If she wanted to ignore me, fine. It creeped me out and I was without a partner, so I wasn't going to press the issue.

With police being dispatched for a manner of issues, it's reasonable to expect that here and there, they may respond to calls of a more supernatural origin. This was the case with the Enfield haunting in London, UK.

In the late 1970s, police responded to a distress call made by Peggy Hodgson, a single mother who lived with her four children in the town of Enfield in north London. Peggy claimed that her children, particularly her two daughters Janet and Margaret, were being tormented by a malevolent entity in their rented home. The disturbances included furniture moving on its own, objects being thrown across the room, and strange knocking sounds coming from the walls. The police initially dismissed it as a prank, but soon witnessed the paranormal activity firsthand, leaving them perplexed and intrigued. Word of the strange occurrences spread quickly, attracting the attention of paranormal investigators and media outlets who were eager to uncover the truth behind the Enfield Poltergeist case.

Before walking away, I tried the doorknob, which is something that is usually disapproved of since it could be seen as a breach of the Fourth Amendment, which safeguards citizens from unjust and unwarranted searches. I couldn't enter the home without a warrant, exigent circumstances, or permission. To my surprise and regret, the door opened. The heavy wooden door creaked as it slowly swung open, eventually hitting the wall with a loud thud.

I shined my light inside. It was definitely an old lady's residence. Everything was lavender and tidy. There were creepy portraits of hairless cats on the walls. There were also statues of them. I reached my hand inside to flick the light on, but it didn't activate. At first, I thought the house had no power. There was no sound of electricity, and it was hotter than a sauna with no airflow. Then I remembered the light upstairs. The whole situation was unsettling.

I dialed my supervisor to get his opinion. I was hoping he would tell me to leave, call the reporting person, and explain what I observed. Before I could dial, I heard a sound that haunts me every night, a chilling noise that will die with me.

You won't believe me, and I don't blame you. It was the sound of intense laughter. Not a giggle, but delirious, gut-busting laughter from what sounded like an old lady. I never drew my Glock faster than I did right then.

"Hello. Who's in the—"

Before I could finish the sentence, it stopped. I'm not too embarrassed to admit that I turned around and sprinted toward my car—my grip tightening around the cold metal of the gun. Just as I left the porch, I was stopped in my tracks. Another equally loud and terrifying noise echoed from the house. This time, it was the scream of someone clearly in distress. It sounded like the same voice, but I wasn't sure.

"Damn," I thought to myself, "exigent circumstances."

I radioed dispatch and told them what I heard. I advised them I would clear the house. Another officer started en route, but I couldn't wait. There was no way I could justify waiting twenty minutes to enter the house of an elderly woman in danger.

Entering the warm living room, I quickly cleared the nearby space. I knew at least one person was upstairs. The narrow staircase led to a pitch-black second floor. Before going up, I announced myself again to no avail.

THE AIR IN THE ROOM WAS HEAVY WITH THE SICKENING SMELL OF DEAD CATS, THEIR SKINNED BODIES CRUELLY DISPLAYED ON WOODEN CROSSES IN EVERY CORNER AND ON EVERY WALL.

I began walking up the staircase as calmly as I could. I remember imagining a scenario where I would be clearing the bedrooms and then Cynthia, the grandmother, would jump out of a dark corner. It would certainly be difficult to explain to the concerned family member why I shot their grandma.

When I was finally upstairs, I checked two rooms that were completely empty. No furniture or anything. It dawned on me that the last bedroom was the one that had the light on. I announced myself and prayed for a response. Without receiving one, I took hold of the doorknob and turned it. The door swung open, and I was immediately met with a nauseating odor. It was the worst I had ever experienced, almost knocking me down.

I illuminated the room with my light. The air in the room was heavy with the sickening smell of dead cats, their skinned bodies cruelly displayed on wooden crosses in every corner and on every wall. Some were rotten, some were fresh. The room was filled with dried blood. Fur and detached claws covered the floor. I dry-heaved as I cleared the closet. It was empty.

I stumbled my way back downstairs, where I vomited on the front porch. I ran to the road to wait for my partner. Once he arrived, we called for even more people and my supervisor. We cleared the house again with no signs of Cynthia.

Fast forward to the next evening. The reporting person flew in with other family members. They searched the 10 or so acres (4 ha) of the property and found an old, abandoned car in the brush. In the passenger seat, her grandma was leaning back, deceased, for what appeared to be several days. Neither detectives nor the medical examiner could determine the cause of death.

Detectives interviewed another family member, who said Cynthia had severe schizophrenia and dementia. Inside her home, in a kitchen drawer, detectives discovered pages and pages of Hebrew writings. The writings translated to devoted allegiances to Baphomet, a devil god that many Satanists worship. Her writings claimed Baphomet asked her to sacrifice her beloved cats.

Opinions differ on whether I actually heard Cynthia laughing and screaming and if the upstairs light was on. Trust me, sometimes I question it myself. For some reason, my body camera never downloaded its footage to the system. It's like it never existed, even though I know it was on. No other calls from that night downloaded either. It even baffled my department.

I have constant nightmares about Cynthia. In them, I hear that all too familiar sinister laughter. She has unusually long fingers and nails that almost scrape the ground when she walks. I never move fast enough to get away from her. I reach for my gun, but it's never there. She always gets me, and then I wake up.

I don't know why I'm still a cop. Maybe it's all I know how to do. I only have twelve more years and many, many more therapy sessions before I can retire. My experience completely changed my perspective on the supernatural—I used to be a skeptic, but not anymore.

To those aspiring to be police officers, heed my advice: Become firefighters instead.

A recent study has revealed that farmers in Spain skinned cats around one thosand years ago. The discovery, at the archaeological site of El Bordellet, was unearthed during highway construction in 2010. As they found other animal remains associated with ritual practices at the site, researchers suggested that skinning the cats could have been for some kind of pagan ritual.

Was this elderly woman attempting to imitate these types of rituals? Or perhaps twist the ritual into something more unholy?

CONCLUSION

As the gnashing of jagged teeth subsides and the harrowing red eyes peering out through the trees begin to shut, it is time for our farewell.

Nearly two decades ago, just trying to kill some time, I began my journey into the dark unknown. My desire was to hear the stories of those who were affected by the bumps in the night we all heard as children.

In this book alone, I have presented you with forty stories of encounters with things we've yet to explain, from the well-known creatures like Bigfoot and werewolves, to more local legends, like monsters that stalk small towns for a quick bite of the local fauna—and even of our fellow man.

And these stories are only a speck of snow on the tip of the iceberg. I am still receiving stories and don't see an end to them anytime soon. I can't help but wonder how many stories have yet to be told. How many encounters were brushed off and explained away? How many people do you pass by every day that might have seen a cup slide across their coffee table seemingly on its own, or witnessed a monster lumbering in the pines?

The fear of judgment prevents numerous individuals from sharing their stories, leaving incredible sights hidden and untold. Stories like the ones you've read are scary and fascinating, but each one has a common element: a survivor.

So, if there is something you come across that you cannot explain, I hope you will take this one message from this book to heart:

You are not alone.

REFERENCES

British Broadcasting Corporation (BBC). www.bbc.com

CBS News. www.cbsnews.com

Encyclopædia Britannica. www.britannica.com

The Guardian. www.theguardian.com

History. www.history.com

NBC News. www.nbcnews.com

ACKNOWLEDGMENTS

None of this would have been possible without the firsthand accounts of the individuals whose stories you've just read, as well as the countless others that have been submitted. It is because of this vibrant community and others like it that the world is filled with such awe-inspiring wonders. We express our sincerest gratitude to the intrepid explorers, the relentlessly curious, and even the unlucky ones for their invaluable contribution in revealing the hidden depths of the world.

The world is brighter for having had you.

A heartfelt thank you to the ever productive and inspiring Carman Carrion, whose passion and hard work are truly inspiring. With her unwavering determination and charm, she has brought countless stories and the individuals who were eager to share them to our doorstep.

We want to express our appreciation to our editor JRT McMahon for lending his skills and enthusiasm to our team.

And of course, thank you to Quarto for the opportunity and dedication assisting us in getting this wonderful collection of horror to the masses.

ABOUT THE AUTHOR

DARKNESS PREVAILS is the online persona of the founder of Eeriecast and host of the podcasts *Unexplained Encounters, Tales from the Break Room,* and *Alone in the Woods* (formerly known as *Outdoor Terrors*).

Darkness lives in the Ozarks, spending his time wrangling two terribly adorable kids and enjoying coyote-filled evenings with his wife. Whenever he's not writing or narrating tales of the creepy and unexplained, he's probably on his computer raging at online video games or working on a card game of his very own.

Darkness discovered his love for ghost stories and cryptids in middle school, where he'd sneak-read online paranormal forums when the computer lab teacher was distracted. Nowadays, if a piece of media isn't horror-adjacent, he simply struggles to sit through it. This writer-turned-podcaster has been narrating allegedly true scary stories since 2015 and has now read and received about ten thousand submissions from real people around the globe.

If Darkness Prevails has one thing to say before you go about your day avoiding the usual nine-to-five terrors, it would be:

"This world is a strange one."

First published in 2024 by Wellfleet Press,
an imprint of The Quarto Group,
142 West 36th Street, 4th Floor,
New York, NY 10018, USA
(212) 779-4972
www.Quarto.com

Wellfleet Press titles are also available at discount for retail, wholesale, promotional, and bulk purchase. For details, contact the Special Sales Manager by email at specialsales@quarto.com or by mail at The Quarto Group, Attn: Special Sales Manager, 100 Cummings Center Suite 265D, Beverly, MA 01915 USA.

10 9 8 7 6 5 4 3 2 1

ISBN: 978-1-57715-433-4

Digital edition published in 2024
eISBN: 978-0-7603-8898-3

Library of Congress Cataloging-in-Publication Data available upon request.

Group Publisher: Rage Kindelsperger
Creative Director: Laura Drew
Editorial Director: Erin Canning
Managing Editor: Cara Donaldson
Editor: Elizabeth You
Art Director: Scott Richardson
Cover Design: Scott Richardson
Interior Design: Silverglass
Additional Tech Edits: JRT McMahon

Printed in China